Truthteller

An investigative reporter's journey through the world of
truth prevention, fake news and conspiracy theories

STEPHEN DAVIS

PUBLISHING

ABOUT THE AUTHOR

Stephen Davis has been on the frontlines of journalism for three decades as an investigative reporter in TV, magazines and newspapers and as a leading journalism educator, trying to uphold the ideals of the fourth estate, and to inspire his students to do the same. From the rainforests of Brazil to the icy wastes of Antarctica, from London to Los Angeles, from the Middle East to Australia and New Zealand, Davis has sought out the truth and sometimes found it. Along the way he has encountered lying politicians and corporate conmen, spies and special forces soldiers, secret policemen and scared scientists. Among those who have tried to dissuade him from reporting his stories: men with Kalashnikovs, government lawyers, corporate PRs in fancy suits, senior police officers, billionaires, and newspaper owners. Davis has worked for *The Sunday Times* in both London and Los Angeles, been a war and foreign correspondent, a TV producer for *60 Minutes* and *20/20*, a newspaper editor, a documentary filmmaker for the BBC and Discovery, and has taught journalism to thousands of students from all over the world. He has won multiple awards for his investigative reporting, including a silver medal at the New York film and television awards, and has designed and run journalism degree programs in London, Sydney and Melbourne. For more about Stephen, visit stephendaviswriter.com.

First published 2019

Exisle Publishing Pty Ltd
226 High Street, Dunedin, 9016, New Zealand
PO Box 864, Chatswood, NSW 2057, Australia
www.exislepublishing.com

A CiP record for this book is available from the National Library of Australia.

ISBN 978 1 925335 89 7

Designed by Nada Backovic
Typeset in 12.5/17pt Perpetua
Printed in China

This book uses paper sourced under ISO 14001 guidelines from well-managed forests and other controlled sources.

10 9 8 7 6 5 4 3 2 1

Disclaimer
This book is based on original investigations undertaken by the author, except where noted or where the work of other journalists has been quoted. All care has been taken in compiling the contents, and neither the author nor the publisher and their distributors can be held responsible for any loss, claim or action that may arise from reliance on the information contained in this book.

Believe in truth. To abandon facts is to abandon freedom.
If nothing is true, then no one can criticize power,
because there is no basis on which to do so.
TIMOTHY SNYDER, HISTORIAN

Truth is relative. They may have a different version
of the truth than we do.
RUDY GIULIANI, DONALD TRUMP'S LAWYER

Contents

Introduction:
A toolbox for lies and deception

The story began with a quote from an anonymous official from the Indian state of Maharashtra. It was reported by the Press Trust of India and then revealed to a wider audience by a Republican congresswoman speaking on CNN. A few hours later it spread all over the internet and the world learnt that President Barack Obama's trip to Asia was going to cost US taxpayers $200 million a day — a staggering $2 billion dollars for the entire ten-day trip. The numbers were huge, and they grew in detail with every new version of the story.

He was taking 2000 people with him — no, it was 3000. Hundreds of hotel rooms had been booked — no, it was 870 — and they were all in five-star hotels like the one at the Taj Mahal. Thirty-four US navy war ships were accompanying the President — later, it was 10 per cent of the entire navy. It was an outrageous waste of government money.

There was just one problem — it wasn't true. It wasn't close to being true, even for those who think there are shades of truth.

The Obama story is an example of the classic political lie: a fabrication spread by Tea Party congresswoman Michele Bachmann, right-wing talk show hosts and online sites. The $200-million-a-day figure was ludicrous — the entire war in Afghanistan, with the deployment of thousands of troops, was costing less than that. Presidential trips do involve large entourages — including a huge security presence — but the cost was more like $5 million per day. The US Navy was going to be there — for exercises with allies — but not 34 ships and not 10 per cent of the navy.

While the true version of the story appeared on traditional media outlets, the false version reached many millions. It was an early example of what might now be called Trumpean falsehoods, after the serially mendacious President of the United States. Blatant lies helped to get him elected and persuaded millions of Americans to support his presidency. These attempts to distort the truth — practised by politicians of all parties and nationalities, to a greater or lesser degree — at least have the merit of being relatively easy to spot, and refute. They are put to the test and exposed by journalists asking the right questions. If you want to find out whether such a story is true, you can.

But there are other forms of government and corporate lying and deception that are harder to spot. There is a large and growing number of methods that the rich, the powerful and the elected use to prevent truth coming out — to bury it, warp it, twist it to suit their purposes. This toolbox of deception is used not only to promote their interests or defeat opponents but to conceal blunders or crimes, to cover up corruption or hide things that are just plain embarrassing.

To show how these tools work, I have used direct examples from my own reporting in stories I have investigated as an award-winning reporter, editor, foreign correspondent, television producer, documentary filmmaker and journalism educator across three decades.

Each chapter begins with the original story, so readers can understand the human consequences of truth denial. In some of these stories there are still questions to be answered and mysteries to be solved, demonstrating how successfully the tools have been deployed. I have also used examples from other media, in case histories. Despite the best efforts of dedicated reporters, the remarkable array of tools used by those in the business of deception continues to be deployed and with great success.

I hope to inspire truth seekers of the future, because the battle between those seeking to expose the truth and those seeking to prevent it is an unequal struggle. Young journalists and other concerned citizens seeking to make informed decisions are up against a huge apparatus of truth denial and distortion.

Journalists, even when working for profitable media companies, have never had the resources of governments and corporations. It is an even more one-sided contest in present-day media, as serious reporting is constrained by finances and the very question of what constitutes journalism, of what *is* a story, is challenged by social media. 'We are all journalists now,' declared one magazine, noting the spread of mobile phone cameras and Twitter accounts. Left unsaid was how anyone was going to verify any of the photos, videos and tweets. So you will also find here a guide to a journalist's decision making — the behind-the-scenes view that you don't often see.

■ ■ ■

Look at what passes for news on any given day. Much of it is trivia that catches people's attention, and often distracts them from what is really going on, things deliberately obscured from view and meant to stay that way. We are bombarded with imagery and words 24/7 in the news cycle — a cycle not just about news, but all kinds of other distractions.

We are on Facebook, watching carefully filtered videos and posts from friends, or YouTube, or discovering 10 Things You Didn't Know

About the Moon Missions via Google. And so all that we read or hear or see has come to seem equally important, or equally unimportant.

Those who have things to hide can hide them in plain sight, a press release or news conference saying X when the real story is actually Y; a public meeting where the discussion they have after they close the doors is about something much more controversial; a corporate video of trees and birds and flowers disguising environmental destruction. Lying, cover-ups, media manipulation — these have always been with us. But now they are practised by ever more skilled, highly paid professionals and, increasingly, zealous amateurs armed with a little knowledge, social media savvy and an agenda.

They know they can get away with it because, well, we simply aren't paying close enough attention. If there is a massacre in Africa and it is not on camera, did it really happen? But a cat on a skateboard, that is real, we can click on that and watch it again and again. We filter things out or let every bit of trivia in; either way, our judgments have become too often the judgments of others. And we wake up every morning in a world where our truth is what we believe on any given day, and if we need a change then a different truth is just a click away. That is a gift for those who would deceive us.

Lie about current events, shout your lies from the rooftops, repeat them again and again with an absolutely straight face and eventually a good proportion of people will believe the lie; and if you can do that often enough, it will help sustain you in power and make it difficult for people to know what is true and what is not. Create your own reality, using your own media, and get the public to believe in that.

Even better, create your own conspiracy, to muddy the waters. People expect to be lied to — give them a conspiracy to suit. Widely read stories tell us how humans did not land on the moon, that the structure of the Louvre in Paris and its pyramid is the key to a secret society, that Mossad organized the attack on the Twin Towers to turn the world against Muslims, and the Bush White House and the CIA helped them do it.

If everything is made to look like a conspiracy then the real conspiracies, the ones that honest journalists have pursued over the years, can easily get lost in the noise. This book is for those who don't want to get lost in the noise. For democracy to function, there needs to be a free flow of facts. There needs to be an understanding that, as American politician Daniel Patrick Moynihan once said, you are entitled to your own *opinions* but you are not entitled to your own *facts*.

Good decision making, either in organizing our own lives or as responsible citizens, is based on accurate information. We must become more critical consumers of the media and for that to happen, we need to be able to recognize the tools that have been used to deceive or to hide things from us.

The historian Timothy Snyder stresses the importance of reality and truth in his cautionary pamphlet, 'On Tyranny'. 'To abandon facts,' he writes, 'is to abandon freedom. If nothing is true, then no one can criticize power because there is no basis upon which to do so. If nothing is true, then all is spectacle. The biggest wallet pays for the most blinding lights.'[1]

The toolbox glossary

There are many tools used to deceive. The deceivers rely on our inattention and our seemingly insatiable demand for the new, so we are often bored with a slow developing story, the steady accumulation of facts. We want instant answers — so unanswered questions are filed away. We lead busy lives so it is difficult to deal with so much detail. Often, we believe the first version of a story and miss the follow-ups. We are all guilty of this and so we are easy victims of some of the major truth-prevention tools described in this book. In some cases, multiple tools are deployed, with variations tailored to suit the lie.

Each chapter of this book describes how one or more of the tools listed below has been used to suppress the truth.

Behind closed doors: let's talk about this

You are accused of wrongdoing, or you or your agency or company has made a mistake or done something embarrassing you wish to hide. Reporters are after you, asking questions you do not wish to answer. You need to make the reporters go away or have the questions asked in such a way that you keep control of the story. You want to frame the questions. Your version of the truth needs to be the one that counts.

So you bypass the reporters and appeal to their editor, or the owners of their media organization, or powerful political or business friends who can put pressure on that organization. You want this sorted out among friends and likeminded people. You want to avoid the messy business of public accountability. You want to discuss the story in secret. You only want to talk behind closed doors.

Deceptions practised by journalists and other good people

Whales are trapped in the ice. An environmental organization has alerted the world to their plight and it has become a big event. The world's media has descended on a remote town in the Arctic.

The story is not what it seems but children all over the world are now hoping the whales are rescued and no one wants to disappoint them. The environmental organization is getting great publicity — the media is getting a great story. So inconvenient facts go unreported. A much more important story in the same town goes unreported. A story like this has to have a happy ending and so that's the story the world hears. Journalists have deceived themselves and the environmental organization has suppressed the truth.

Delay delay delay, until everyone gets bored

A 21-year-old Avis employee is sitting in the car park where he works. Alongside him is another man who might have reason to harm him. Later, the 21-year-old man disappears. He is never seen again. A man walks into a local police station and says he wants to confess to the murder of the missing man. A senior detective is informed but he does not rush to the station to take the confession. It's the weekend. Two days later there is still no confession. Years go by. The missing person's case remains unsolved. The missing man's mother tries to get the investigation re-opened but nothing happens.

Finally there is an inquest in which questions are raised about police misconduct. The original officer is now a very senior man in the force. Nothing happens; the alleged killer moves to another country and more years pass. It's now an old story. The delaying tactics have worked. There is nothing new to say and journalists stop asking questions.

Intimidation: shoot the messengers

In the Amazon, a huge mining operation is destroying the rainforest and poisoning the local water supply. The mine is owned by one of the world's largest companies, which boasts of its green credentials. The destruction is hidden from view, protected by armed guards and by its remoteness. A group of honest forestry service officials helps a reporter reach the mine and expose what is going on there.

But the mining company has influence in high places. The government reacts not by investigating the claims of destruction but by attacking those who helped the journalist, threatening their livelihoods. It is an effective tactic, preventing the story from prompting any lasting change and making others fearful of helping journalists to expose other destructive operations in the Amazon. The truth is lost in the forest.

Faraway places of which we know little: the value of distance

There is a daring rescue in the icy wastes of Antarctica. An Air Force Hercules flies in. The heroic midwinter flight — in total darkness and with a temperature low enough to freeze the plane's oil and fuel within minutes — gets worldwide coverage. But who was rescued and why?

Journalists begin asking questions. There is surprising level of secrecy and wild rumours: of nuclear accidents, of patients with burns. Sources give out information and then deny giving any. Officials provide contradictory details. Everyone acts like there is something to hide.

But the truth remains elusive. The Antarctic is far away and impossible to get to without official permission. It is a territory controlled by no nation. Operations there, scientific and otherwise, are not well understood. Journalists cannot do the one thing that they would do on other stories closer to home: go to the scene and start asking questions.

Even in the internet age, distance still counts. The story just goes away.

Laughter, disinformation and other weapons: the art of character assassination

A spy is sacked by his country's intelligence services for reasons that are unclear. He is denied any right of appeal. He tries to write a book about his time as a spy; the government tries to stop him. He is pursued around the world, sometimes through the courts but also by other means. He is beaten up by French police in Paris, held in chains in New York, strip-searched in Auckland, accused of being a paedophile in Geneva. He is accused of leaking the names of MI6 agents. His theories are dismissed as a joke. Anonymous government sources feed negative stories about him to journalists. A tabloid newspaper calls him a traitor and publishes his email address. He receives death threats.

He becomes not someone dismissed in dubious circumstances from a job he loved but a rogue peddler of wild stories and, at the same time, a threat to national security. The intelligence service is not held accountable. The whistleblower is silenced.

Manufacture another truth

Imagine a planeload of passengers on your national airline has been flown into a war zone. They have been taken away in buses from an airport surrounded by tanks. They are in the hands of a hostile power run by a bloodthirsty dictator. Journalists are asking questions about why the plane was allowed to land. Your government had a team of undercover soldiers and spies on board and they don't want the media to discover that. What are they to do?

The government doesn't know what will happen to the passengers or whether their lives are at risk. But they do know that they have temporarily been taken to a group of luxury hotels. These hotels have pools and cocktail bars. It is sunny. Perfect. Spokespeople brief journalists anonymously that the passengers are safe and well and are relaxing in the finest hotels, probably sipping cocktails by the pool. It is a temporary disruption, more like an unexpected holiday. The journalists' concerns are diverted for now. They move on to other urgent events.

It is not quite a lie. They have simply manufactured another truth.

Official secrets and other means of suppression

A special forces soldier on a secret mission is wounded and captured. After release he is angered to discover that senior officers decided not to try to rescue him and his fellow patrol members. He quits in disgust, but before he leaves he is forced to sign a lifelong non-disclosure contract. He is not allowed legal advice.

He wants to write a book about the mission just as other books have been written. The government decides his version of events should not be published. They deploy their contract as a weapon. They pursue him at home and even to the country of his birth, 19,200 kilometres (11,900 miles) away. Expensive lawyers are deployed at huge cost and appeal after appeal is lodged. They try to ruin him.

The government loses but it keeps on going. Eventually it wins the right to take all the soldier's profits. The book is published but by now it is old news. They have put the solider through hell — to discourage any others.

Our conspiracy theories are better than yours

A ferry sinks in one of the worst shipping disasters in history. There are serious questions about why it sank — was it an accident or deliberate? Governments promise to spare no expense to bring the sunken ferry to the surface. But then they do the opposite: they try to bury the wreck. Evidence emerges that a hostile foreign power may have been responsible for the sinking.

Journalists suspect a conspiracy but key questions are never answered. As time goes on, new conspiracy theories emerge which point in other directions. Some of them originate from the hostile power. More conspiracy theories are floated, each more bizarre and unlikely than the last. Some of them are promoted by extremists on the internet.

By now, who can really tell the difference between all the theories floating round in cyberspace, between legitimate journalists asking serious questions and the crazies with plausible-looking websites? The ferry remains buried, along with the truth.

State-sponsored stories and other distractions

You are the leader of a nuclear power. There is an enemy of state you want killed. You send your spies to poison him, along with his daughter. The poison is traced back to your country, which is blamed for the killing. No matter, you issue firm denials. And your diplomats, trolls and bots, and friendly media deliver a host of alternative explanations for what happened. It's a plot to embarrass your country. They weren't really poisoned — they have been abducted and hidden away. Or they were poisoned but it was a different poison and not from your country. Or they simply fell ill from something they caught locally. You even deploy an old favourite: the Israelis did it.

It doesn't matter how credible the stories are because now there are at least a dozen different theories about what happened and you have succeeded in planting doubt in the minds of many.

And the ultimate truth-prevention tool: create your own reality and get millions of people to believe you

Take a fact that supports something you are trying to do and twist it out of all recognition. If that fails, just make it up. Get yourself quoted on friendly media and have them run with the story. Then get other friendly media to quote them. Then you quote the friendly media in support of the story, and then the story spreads on the internet through 'news' sites and Twitter.

You refer to the story, and how it is spreading, again and again, as evidence that it is true. This provides another story for the friendly media and then you mention their 'new' report and they quote you and the whole cycle begins again. If other reporters challenge your version of events, just label their reporting as Fake News. Your supporters will believe you. They have already heard the story from multiple sources that they trust and they believe it.

You have created your own reality.

1. From the toolbox:
The art of character assassination

THE STRANGE JOURNEY OF RICHARD TOMLINSON

IN THE NEWS, 7 DECEMBER 2014

**Aston Martin DB10 revealed as
James Bond's new ride
Typhoon kills two in Philippines
NASA probe approaches Pluto
US ban may ground MI6 whistleblower**

Richard Tomlinson is lying on a bed in a cheap hotel on the Rue d'Amsterdam, just around the corner from the Gare St Lazare, the busy Paris railway terminus with its grand nineteenth-century façade. It is mid-afternoon, 3.30 p.m., and he needs a break. It had been a stressful 24 hours. He was thirsty and he had bought a bottle of Evian water before going up to his room. There is a knock on the door, a loud knock.

'*Que désirez-vous?*' What you do want? Tomlinson calls.

'*C'est la réception,*' a male voice answers.

Tomlinson gets up, walks to the door and unlocks it. As soon as he turns the key, three men who look like front-row forwards in a French rugby team burst through the door, knocking him to the ground. They are shouting 'police, police' as they leap on him. Punches rain down on the back of his head. They pull his arms behind his back and handcuff him.

As he lies prone one of them kicks him — a savage kick that breaks a rib. The punches continue even after he is cuffed and stop only when he stops moving. Tomlinson looks up to see two other men behind the heavies who had burst in. They have revolvers and are pointing their weapons at his head.

Richard John Charles Tomlinson, formerly of Gonville and Caius College, Cambridge University, holder of a first-class honours degree in aeronautical engineering, a Kennedy scholarship winner to the Massachusetts Institute of Technology and a former officer of the Secret Intelligence Service, MI6, lies still. He does not want to give the men with the guns an excuse to fire. He is completely at their mercy.

■ ■ ■

In Manchester two weeks earlier a confident and cheerful Tomlinson had met me along with a television current affairs team at the Gardens Hotel at 55 Piccadilly. It was a meeting that had been planned for months and we were there to discuss Tomlinson returning to New Zealand, the land of his birth, to be interviewed for the current affairs program I worked on. He also wanted to check out job opportunities there. That night, we had wandered around Manchester through pubs, clubs and back streets until Tomlinson, who had been trained by counter-surveillance experts at Fort Monkton in Portsmouth, was confident we were not being followed.

As we were checking in at the hotel he produced his wallet and I noticed ID and credit cards in more than one name. He saw I had noticed and turned to me with a shrug. 'You know, one of the difficulties is remembering who you are supposed to be at any one time.'

Who exactly the real Richard Tomlinson was — whistleblower, malcontent, fantasist, a pervert, a hero exposing misconduct or a threat to national security and the lives of his fellow agents — was to prove difficult to answer. He was to be the subject of a huge and expensive government campaign of truth suppression that lasted many years.

The Tomlinson who worked as an officer for MI6 seemed to be a long-time high flyer. He had been tapped on the shoulder at Cambridge and invited to join the SIS, the Secret Intelligence Service, better known as MI6. (In World War II, one of its names was military intelligence, section 6. The name stuck.)

At first he refused and took a job in the corporate sector at consultants Booz Allen Hamilton. He joined the UK's volunteer army reserve, known as the Territorial Army, in a part-time unit attached to the Special Air Service (the SAS), where he completed basic training and got his parachute wings. At 27, he decided that the life of a civilian and part-time soldier was not for him and joined MI6. He passed his training course at Fort Monkton with top marks and became an intelligence officer.

SPY OR INTELLIGENCE OFFICER?

Thanks to James Bond and other literary and Hollywood fictions, the public has become familiar with the designation 'spy' or 'secret agent'. In fact, people who work for MI6 are called intelligence officers and those who recruit people overseas are agent runners or case officers — the CIA's preferred term. They are not spies. It's the people they recruit, whom they persuade to betray their own country to obtain valuable information deemed essential to national security, who are the spies or agents.

Just a few months later, while still on probation, Tomlinson found himself on a mission to Moscow, the toughest place in the world for a western intelligence officer to operate. He was using the cover name Alex Huntley, working for a company interested in East European investment. Much of the work was mundane, attending conferences and having meetings to maintain his cover. In his book, *The Big Breach*, he described one of his days.

> *That morning I attended the last lectures at the Metropol. Future Prime Minister, Victor Chernomyrdin, then head of Gazprom, was the star speaker. Several members of the British embassy came to listen. I scribbled a few jottings in my notebook to keep up my cover, but didn't pay too much attention to the content of the lectures. My mind was on the job ahead.*

After a quick lunch, I hurried to my room, locked the door firmly and removed a WH Smith pad of A4 notepaper from my briefcase. The first 20 pages or so were filled with the notes I had taken from the conference — junk that would be discarded in London. At the back of the pad, I carefully ripped out the fifth-to-last page, took it to the bathroom, placed it on the plastic lid of the toilet seat and removed a bottle of Ralph Lauren Polo Sport aftershave from my spongebag. Moistening a small wad of cotton wool with the doctored aftershave, I slowly and methodically wiped it over the surface of the paper.

In a matter of seconds, the large Russian script of SOU's handwriting started to show, slowly darkening to a deep pink. Using the hotel hair dryer I carefully dried the damp sheet, trying not to wrinkle it too much and driving away the strong smell of perfume. It now looked like a normal handwritten letter, though in a slightly peculiar dark red ink. Reaching into the back of my supplied briefcase, I pulled on the soft calfskin lining, ripping apart the Velcro fastening it to the outer casing, slipped the paper into the small gap and resealed it. It would take a very diligent search to find the hidden pocket.[1]

The man codenamed SOU was a Russian defector, and the letter contained instructions for Tomlinson's mission. He'd had little field experience and had been warned that there was no point in an inexperienced officer like himself attempting anti-surveillance in the Russian capital. The Russians had decades of practice. It took at least six months in the city before a new officer could reliably spot the tails.

Tomlinson did run basic anti-surveillance as he travelled on the Moscow metro on the way to the suburb of Zelenograd — that involved techniques like using staircases that switched back on themselves, subways under busy main roads and walking through shopping malls. In Zelenograd, he arrived at a dark green apartment block in a soulless housing estate like so many on the outskirts of the city. 'The rubbish strewn entrance lobby stank of piss and vomit and was covered in graffiti. I pushed the button to call the lifts more out of hope than expectation. MI6's source had told me it hadn't worked for years.'

Tomlinson walked up to the eighth floor and knocked on the door of apartment 82A. An old lady answered. He spoke to her in Russian: 'My name is Alex. I am a friend of your daughter and son-in-law in England. I have a letter for you.'

The old lady made a cup of strong, heavily sugared black tea then went and collected books, clothes and knick-knacks belonging to his source, SOU, for Tomlinson to take with him. When she returned to the kitchen he saw a sewing box that SOU had described. Inside were two light blue school exercise books. They were filled with row upon row of numbers.

He returned to the Metropol Hotel lugging a heavy box containing the precious notebooks and the other possessions. The next morning he rang the British embassy and asked to visit the commercial section's library to get information on East European investment. At the embassy, directly opposite the Kremlin, he showed the receptionist his passport under the name Huntley.

The embassy worked under the assumption that every room was bugged except for the MI6 secure room, which was electronically protected. The other assumption was that all the staff employed locally — clerks, drivers and cleaners — were all reporting back to Russian intelligence. So Tomlinson maintained his Huntley cover within the embassy, even as he met his MI6 contact and handed over the precious notebooks. They were later sent to London via diplomatic bag.

The notebooks contained critical details on the flight paths of every ballistic missile fired from the test range in Kamchatka over a four-year period. SOU, a colonel in the Strategic Rocket Forces who had defected to Britain, had noted down all the numbers in the exercise books after each test flight and the numbers would help experts understand the accuracy and range of the missiles. The information was later passed to the CIA, where it was used in studies to improve anti-ballistic missile defences.

HOW DO YOU TELL IF AN INTELLIGENCE OPERATION IS A SUCCESS?

There are many difficulties for a reporter covering the intelligence services. One is writing about successful operations or failures. The world of intelligence was once memorably described by CIA spycatcher James Angleton as a 'wilderness of mirrors'. Simply put, even top professionals can have trouble working out what is real and what is not, whether they are being deceived or told the truth, even whether an operation is successful or not.

Intelligence services only rarely talk about their successes — that's left to the politicians — and almost never about their failures. What information there is usually reaches the public via the media, and that comes from a reporter's carefully cultivated sources. But even here there are traps

— trusted sources can, for political reasons, mislead journalists. This happened when the *New York Times* was fed dubious information on Saddam Hussein's weapons of mass destruction as the Bush White House made the case for invading Iraq.

Then there are operations that may be successful at the time but lead to long-term failures. An example is the CIA providing weapons to the Mujahideen in Afghanistan to fight the Soviets. The Russians were forced to leave Afghanistan but later those same weapons and the trained and hardened fighters were used against the West. Of course, in the secret world, the most successful operations are by definition the ones you never hear about, unless something goes badly wrong.

One of the most successful intelligence operations of all time involved an Israeli agent called Eli Cohen. Cohen worked for Mossad, the Israeli secret service. He set himself up in Syria working undercover as a businessman and developed extraordinary relationships with political and military leaders. He was so successful that he became an adviser to the Syrian ministry of defence. The intelligence he obtained helped Israel win the Six Day War.

Cohen's operation could have gone on for years until he was brought out and left to enjoy a comfortable retirement. To protect their methods and the intelligence they gained, Mossad would have kept the secret, perhaps forever. But Cohen was careless in his radio transmissions and was caught red-handed by Syrian counter-intelligence. It was only at that point, where a success had turned into a failure, that Israel went public in negotiations to get him home. It did not work. Cohen was tortured and publicly hanged in Marjeh Square in Damascus.

There will be other Cohens working for the world's intelligence services, their operations hidden from public view. Equally, successful cyber-spying — listening to your enemy's communications — is never voluntarily disclosed. Even after the whistleblower Edward Snowden revealed secret files of the NSA, the National Security Agency in the US, no journalist or intelligence analyst could judge for certain the scope of the surveillance. Experts could not even agree how much damage he had done to NSA operations.

The media need to report on intelligence services or there would be no accountability at all. But the honest answer to the question of a journalist investigating intelligence successes or failures is that you can never be entirely sure. You just have to trust your sources — and hope you don't get burnt.

In the case of Tomlinson's mission to Moscow, we only learnt of it through his book. We don't really know how valuable the mission was. It would not be in the interests of either MI6 or the CIA for the Russians to know exactly what was on the notebooks brought out of Moscow, or to what extent it helped the West. But Tomlinson's account of what happened has never been challenged by M16 and has been confirmed by other sources, so we can reasonably assume it is accurate.

The Moscow mission was quite a coup for the young intelligence officer. But only three years later, Richard Tomlinson was dismissed from the service without any right of appeal. Tomlinson walked into MI6 headquarters at Vauxhall Cross in London in April 2005 and swiped his security card. Three times he tried and each time got a red light, not a green. Guards appeared and took him into a watch room. They punched his details into the computer and told him his pass had been cancelled. He was escorted to the personnel department on the eighth floor and told he had been sacked, effective immediately. The service would find him a job — 'something in the City'. He was told to go home and not to return. 'The service refused to give any reasons,' Tomlinson says, other than such generalities as he was not a team player and lacked commitment. He found the commitment claim ridiculous as he had just completed a difficult and dangerous assignment in Bosnia in the middle of the civil war, for which he had been praised. It was a grim assignment — he had seen people killed in front of him — and he also had to cope with the death of his girlfriend from cancer. Now he found himself unemployed, out on the street with just three months' pay, and with the service refusing to put in writing the reasons for his dismissal, on the grounds that to commit them to paper would be a breach of the Official Secrets Act.

Tomlinson attempted to take his employers to an industrial tribunal on the grounds of unfair dismissal. He was seeking reinstatement with full pay. MI6 blocked this by issuing a Public Interest Immunity Certificate. A PIC is a gagging order — an officially approved truth-suppression tool. The certificate can be issued by a government minister — in this case the then Foreign Secretary Malcolm Rifkind — and it prevents courts from hearing evidence and reading documents on the grounds of there being a threat to national security. It is the government that defines what is in the public interest and what constitutes a threat to national security. The certificate gives

**Foreign &
Commonwealth
Office**

15 October 1997

Personnel Services Department
Room 3.1.2
1 Palace Street
London SW1E 3HZ

Telephone: 0171-238 4817
Facsimile: 0171-238 4046

PRIVATE AND CONFIDENTIAL

<u>To Whom It May Concern</u>

Richard John Charles Tomlinson

Richard Tomlinson joined the fast stream of HM Diplomatic Service in September 1991 with extensive travel and work experience, having spent time in four continents: Asia, Europe, Africa and America (North and South). He had a strong scientific background, which included a First in Aeronautical Engineering from the University of Cambridge and a Master's from the Massachusetts Institute of Technology (MIT). He possessed a pilot's licence, was an active sportsman and had a wide range of sporting interests. Those responsible for staff selection noted his drive, energy, interest and determination. They assessed that he was able to motivate himself and had the potential to plan and organise for others.

In his work in London he demonstrated above average qualities of penetration, decisiveness, reliability under pressure, creativity, foresight and resourcefulness. From December 1993 to July 1994, he was posted as Civil Adviser to the Commander of the British Forces in Bosnia. This assignment required him to establish working relationships with a wide range of groups and authorities, civilian and military and of various nationalities, and doing so in several languages. His staff responded well to his management style and appreciated his willingness to spend much of his spare time with them.

After July 1994 he was once more employed in London where his performance was assessed as good. However, consideration of the long term options led eventually to a decision that a career in the Diplomatic Service did not suit Mr Tomlinson and he left the Service in September 1995.

Yours faithfully

Colin Milton
Personnel Officer
Personnel Services Department

*A glowing reference produced by MI6 to help Tomlinson find a new job.
Note the pretence that he was working in the Diplomatic Service.*

extraordinary power and almost no accountability. British appeal courts right up to the law lords have upheld government's rights to issue the certificates.

For Tomlinson, it meant his case could not even be heard in a closed court without members of the public or journalists present, even though 'my personnel papers contained no more secrets than the papers of an employee of the gas board'. He went next to the civil liberties organization Liberty, which took up his case without success. He managed to appeal to the Intelligence Services Tribunal, a panel of three senior judges who had the power to examine the legality of actions by MI6. The panel had been given documents about Tomlinson by the security service but, extraordinarily, he was not allowed to see them at the hearing. What they had written about him could not be challenged.

It is hard to imagine a more fundamental breach of the principles of natural justice. It might as well have been a trial in the old Soviet Union. Tomlinson was in financial difficulties. No good job offers had materialized, despite the promises of help. At one stage he was reduced to earning some cash as a motorcycle dispatch rider. The tribunal, predictably, ruled in favour of MI6. With his legal avenues blocked and no money, Tomlinson decided to write a book about his experiences. He slipped out of the country using his false passport in the name Alex Huntley, with his real passport, driver's licence and cash hidden in a bottle in the petrol tank of his Honda motorbike. After drifting through France and Spain, he ended up in the town of Fuengirola on the Spanish coast, and began to write. His battle with the British government was about to escalate.

■■■

In the 1980s a former MI5 officer, Peter Wright, wrote a book called *Spycatcher*. MI5's job was to catch spies operating in the United Kingdom while MI6 recruited agents abroad to spy for Britain. The government embarked on a long and disastrous attempt to stop the book being published. I met Wright in Australia, where he had gone to get his book published. Unlike other spies I had met, he was a fairly boring character, obsessed by the fact that the Brits had not paid him a proper pension. It was clear that if he had got a decent pension, he never would have written the book. He was also a racist. He told me he had gone to live in Tasmania rather than other Australian states because 'there were fewer blacks'.

The British government lost its attempt to ban the book in Australia, through the skilled efforts of Malcolm Turnbull, his lawyer, who later became prime minister. The British case was not helped by a disastrous appearance on the witness stand by the distinguished civil servant Sir Robert Armstrong, the cabinet secretary. Armstrong was forced to admit that he had been economical with the truth. That is, he had lied. Apparently it was meant as a joke but it backfired badly. Despite their failure in Australia, the government carried on attempting to block publication. They took out multiple injunctions in English courts even though the book was available in Scotland. People were smuggling copies through Heathrow, Gatwick and Manchester airports.

The Economist summed up the absurdity with a blank page and the comment: 'In all but one country, our readers have on this page a review of *Spycatcher*, a book by an ex-MI5 man, Peter Wright. The exception is Britain, where the book, and comment on it, has been banned. For our 420,000 readers there, this page is blank — and the law is an ass.'

Eventually the government admitted defeat and allowed publication. They had turned *Spycatcher* into a bestseller. A dull book ended up selling more than 2 million copies. The British establishment had lost a battle but they were determined to apply the lessons of defeat. They would not lose the war against journalists and other people who wanted to write about the secret world. They passed a new Official Secrets Act, with major adjustments to the previous version, aimed directly at former spooks.

Under the Official Secrets Act 1989, there was now an absolute lifelong prohibition on revelations by serving or former intelligence officers. As he sat in his Spanish bedsit writing, Tomlinson was breaching the Act with every word. His defiance was to be a key test of the new powers of suppression — and the effectiveness of a much older tool, that of character assassination. An example was to be made of him, to discourage others.

MI6 tracked Tomlinson to his hideout in Spain and sent Spanish police to interview him. Later, after meeting him in Madrid, MI6 offered him a deal. Tomlinson would be found a job and helped with his finances — a £15,000 loan — and there was a promise not to prosecute if he returned to the UK. For this, he had to cease his demands to take his case to an employment tribunal, and give MI6 the copyright to anything he wrote. He was told that if he didn't sign, his safety could not be guaranteed. He signed the deal but immediately regretted it. The job that had been arranged was with the Jackie Stewart motor racing team at substantially lower pay and lower status than he had earnt as an intelligence officer, so he felt they were not living up to their end of the bargain.

During a visit to Australia, looking for new opportunities (as an NZ passport holder he had the right to work in Australia) he had discussed writing a book with the publisher Transworld but that did not proceed. Now matters came to a head. Unhappy with his new job, Tomlinson poked the bear. He wrote to MI6 asking how he would go about getting a manuscript approved for publication. MI6 obtained a statement from his publisher outlining the discussion of the proposed book, and arrested him. He was charged with breaching Section 1 of the Official Secrets Act. He was held on remand, then tried in a case largely heard behind closed doors, and found guilty.

He was jailed for six months as a category A (high security) prisoner in HM Prison Belmarsh, in south London, where he served his time alongside the kind of people whom he might have run operations against, such as members of active service units of the IRA, the Irish Republican Army. He did not come out of Belmarsh repenting his sins. 'All the six months of boring frustration had succeeded in doing was increasing my resolve to publish this book,' he wrote.

I was a producer for Television New Zealand and they agreed that we would try to get Tomlinson out for an interview. The thinking was that, back in his country of birth with a free press and court system that had a reputation for independence, we could get his story to air. We would be literally a world away from the Official Secrets Act. After meeting him in Manchester, we returned to New Zealand to await his arrival. He had sent his NZ passport to the embassy in Paris and he went to France to collect it, the first stage of his journey to Auckland. But it turned out that New Zealand was not quite as independent as we imagined. The long-standing intelligence relationship between

New Zealand and the UK (there is an intelligence-sharing agreement that also includes the United States, Canada and Australia) trumped any questions of individual freedom.

We received an ominous fax from Tomlinson (he had decided fax was a more secure form of information than phone or email):

FAX TRANSMISSION

TO: Steven Davis
FAX: 00 64 9 375 0778

FROM: Richard Tomlinson
TEL: 00 33 1 42 85 36 36 (room 503)
FAX: 00 33 1 42 85 16 93
PAGES: 1 (including this)

Dear Steven,

Just a quick note to let you know where I am. I slipped out of the UK without a passport a few days before the end of my probation, because I was certain that MI6 were planning on illegally preventing me from leaving the UK once they were obliged to return my passport. As I told you, they already tried to rearrest me for not surrendering my NZ passport, but luckily the probation service would not allow them to do this. However, from August 1, I would not have the protection of the (legally accountable) probation service, and my fear was that MI6 would find another pretext to (illegally) rearrest me and so stop me from leaving the UK.

I am now staying at a Hotel in Paris, and am trying to get the NZ Embassy here to give me back my passport and allow me to return to NZ. The Paris consular official (Kevin Bonici) is being very reasonable, and sees no reason why my passport should not be immediately returned, as I have never broken any French or New Zealand law. However, MI6 are putting pressure on both the London High Commission and even on Wellington to not return my passport. The fact that MI6 have gone to the lengths to contact Wellington over this just goes to show that my hunch that they were planning something against me was probably correct. If this was not the case, why are they so concerned about me leaving the UK a few days early? I am also intrigued to learn that Wellington appear, at the moment, to be listening to MI6. I thought Wellington was independent of London now!

Anyway, please feel free to contact me on the above number at anytime. I am in and out all day, so you may have to try a couple of times. I have sent this fax to Rod, but thought I had better also copy you in case he was away on assignment.

Yours sincerely,

Richard Tomlinson

MI6 had arranged for Tomlinson to be arrested by French police and roughed up. He was held for questioning for 38 hours and two officers from Special Branch in London came to join the interrogation. Eventually the French decided they could not hold him, and he was able to collect his New Zealand passport and fly to Auckland, only to find an injunction waiting for him as he stepped out of the customs hall and on to New Zealand soil. It turned out that despite Tomlinson's anti-surveillance efforts, we had been followed the whole time we were in Manchester.

We were able to broadcast only a bland interview with no new information. Our legal predicament as the new target of the British truth-suppression strategy was summed up in an Internal TVNZ memo, which outlined the threat:

The News Media / Steve Davis

The details of Tomlinson's experiences have not been previously released, so the defence of previous publication would not be available.

Davis is on notice that any information passed along by Tomlinson has the potential to be a violation of the Official Secrets Act in Britain, and he knows that the British government has taken steps to protect it.

Ten years after Spycatcher, a New Zealand court may be less willing to say that the secrets of the United Kingdom are necessarily of public interest to the citizens of New Zealand.

The link between the news media and the disgruntled security service agent here would be direct, so it would be easier to argue that the duty of confidentiality has passed to Davis.

If a valid injunction covers any release of this information in New Zealand, then Davis could be held in contempt for the release and fined. It appears that contempt charges are the only remedy of the Crown, though the Mutual Assistance in Criminal Matters Act may be implemented to seize items in Davis's possession.

Much of this would be left to the discretion of the court, and the issue may in the end turn on how much of its political clout the New Zealand government is willing to risk to maintain good intelligence agency relations with the United Kingdom.

Tomlinson headed off to Australia, hoping to find friendlier territory. Tomlinson was not allowed to settle in Australia, after pressure from the UK government who pursued him relentlessly, around the world, from Auckland and Sydney to Singapore and Bangkok. Attempting to enter the US, he was arrested at JFK airport and held in chains before being put back on a plane. Munich was his next stop, then Zurich. He was arrested multiple times and then released. The chasing included short trips to Italy and Monte Carlo. Dozens of officers from the intelligence services and police of at least ten countries were deployed against him and the time and money spent is incalculable.

In the meantime, MI6's attempts to blacken his name continued. They told Swiss police that he was a paedophile, a claim for which there was no supporting evidence whatsoever. But the anti-Tomlinson campaign was paying off in the media. Reports began to refer to him as a rogue and a traitor.

There were still those sympathetic to his cause, however. That changed when the Press Association in the UK received an official message from Rear Admiral David Pulvertaft, who had the very British title of secretary of the Defence, Press and Broadcasting Advisory Committee. The Pulvertaft message was what was known as a D notice, a profoundly undemocratic device where a committee issues advisory notices to the media — advice treated as instructions — not

('<,:'?

(:,tJ TH E HIGH COURT OF NEW ZEALAND
, ˥]) W ELLINGTONREGISTRY
ςιι

CP No. 220/98

BETWEEN   HER MAJESTY'S ATTORNEY-GENERAL FOR
ENGLAND AND WALES,

Plaintiff

A N D   RICHARD TOMLINSON, formerly of England but now of
parts unknown

Defendant

JUDGMENT AGAINST DEFENDANT
Dated 8 September 1999

UPON reading the statement of claim
and the interlocutory application for
judgment by the plaintiff and the
affidavits of David Arthur Laurenson
and Edward James Grove and upon
hearing B W F Brown QC and F M
Tweedie, counsel on behalf of the
plaintiff, there being no appearance on
behalf of the defendant, the Court
orders:

That an injunction issue restraining the defendant whether by himself, his servants or agents or otherwise howsoever from disclosing to any newspaper or other organ of the media or to any other person otherwise howsoever any information obtained by him in the course of or by virtue of his employment in and position as a member of the Secret Intelligence Service whether in relation to the work of or in support of, the security intelligence services or otherwise."

An example of the draconian nature of the many court injunctions taken out against Tomlinson. A decision made in his absence, and without any legal representation on his behalf. Of course, the judge finds against him — and also issues an order for costs against him — for $NZ10,000.

to publish something or other said to threaten national security. Such notices were produced in secret and delivered to the media — often without the media reporting they had received a D notice. There was no official means of checking whether or not the claims were true.

The notice warned about a list just published on the internet naming 115 serving MI6 officers around the world, with their dates of birth and postings. It looked like a catastrophe for British intelligence — their officers' names revealed to all, lives threatened, careers derailed, operations compromised. (Among the names was that of Moscow-based Christopher Steele, now best known as the author of the controversial dossier on President Donald Trump's links to Russia.) The list was published on a website belonging to conspiracy theorist and past US presidential candidate Lyndon LaRouche, but Tomlinson was blamed.

The Guardian newspaper in the UK reported:

> *Britain's secret intelligence service, MI6, was thrown into unprecedented disarray last night when a renegade former officer published the names of over 100 agents — some said to be false — on the internet.*
>
> *The names on the website were provided by Richard Tomlinson, the former MI6 officer now living in Switzerland. Government lawyers were last night frantically trying to close down the site as senior MI6 officers were mounting a desperate damage-limitation exercise.*
>
> *Mr Tomlinson had recently warned MI6 he would publish the names of his former colleagues on the internet ...*[2]

Tomlinson denied he had released the list. The government's attempt to put a lid on it backfired. Journalists queued up to interview him and the story for a while descended into farce. When the BBC attempted to find out the truth about the list, they called on Legal Affairs correspondent Joshua Rozenberg. He flew to meet Tomlinson in Geneva. 'I knew he would deny having anything to do with the names that had been published; he had done so already,' Rozenberg wrote. 'But how could I find out if he was telling the truth?' He continued:

> The person who had compiled the original list had added a pithy epithet to the name of one particular individual. The list's author presumably knew this particular intelligence officer and apparently had little regard for him.
>
> I copied the name on to a card and showed it to Richard Tomlinson. Did he know that man? He hesitated before answering. 'Yes, I do know him,' he said.
>
> What do you know about him? At this point, Mr Tomlinson's memory started to fade. He did not really know anything about the person on the card. He did not remember him at all well. The man was not anyone he had any great dealings with. He could not say whether the abusive remark was an apt description.[3]

Tomlinson later explained that he could not say he knew the name of the man on the card because that would be a breach of the Official Secrets Act. Rosenberg's story ended with a twist. 'When I got home I decided to check exactly what Mr Tomlinson had said. The computer disc on which I had made an audio recording of the interview turned out to be completely blank. Spooky, or what?'

The damage to Tomlinson's reputation was done. The tabloid *Sun* newspaper published his private email address, which led to death threats.

I have a copy of the infamous list. Many of those named on it were retired or declared — that is, their status as MI6 officers had been declared to the countries they were working in. It was a list that appeared more damaging than it actually was, on the surface. No one to this day has ever confirmed who leaked it.

■ ■ ■

Nothing from Richard Tomlinson's time as an intelligence officer seemed to reveal any state secrets and the information he held was years out of date. But from MI6's point of view, an intelligence service could not function properly if officers went off to write books about their missions. To this end, they deployed the tools of character assassination — variously portraying him as a threat and a joke.

The British government and its agencies were quite prepared to feed false stories about him to journalists and to persuade the police forces and intelligence services of many countries to harass him, time that could have been spent going after terrorists and criminals. They were prepared to spend millions of pounds of taxpayers' money on lawyers as they pursued him through the courts.

In one important way, the toolbox worked — to this day, no other MI6 officer has tried to break ranks and go public. But as far as Tomlinson was concerned, their efforts only succeeded in publicizing his story, turning him into an attractive interviewee for journalists as they had done with *Spycatcher*. They would have been better off allowing him to challenge his dismissal in an industrial tribunal. They certainly misjudged their man. Their attempts to silence him failed. Each time they attacked him he pushed back.

After being blocked from interviewing Tomlinson at TVNZ, I became determined to get him on camera for a full interview. Taking advantage of the fact that I was now working not at TVNZ but at its commercial competitor, TV3, and with legal advice that the injunction probably no longer applied to me, I tracked him down to the south of France.

We were followed to our meeting by men whom I assumed were from French intelligence or the police. It was overt surveillance, the kind where they want you to know they are watching you. In Nice, we talked to Tomlinson about his time at MI6 and his life afterward, and a couple of sensational claims he had made regarding the death of Princess Diana in the infamous car crash in Paris.

There were reports that Henri Paul, the driver, deputy head of security at the Hotel Ritz, had crashed in the underpass because he'd been blinded by a mysterious flash of light. Tomlinson said he had once seen an MI6 plan to kill Serbian leader Slobodan Milošević by blinding his driver with a bright light.

Tomlinson also told me he knew for a fact that Henri Paul, who was intoxicated at the time of the accident, was an MI6 asset. He knew from past experience that when assets met their agent runners, there was generally a lot of drinking. Paul had been drinking before the fatal drive. Tomlinson speculated that he had met his handler who had plied him with alcohol in which case MI6 would have every reason to cover up any involvement in the accident.

Although Tomlinson had been quoted elsewhere as strongly pushing these claims, in our broadcast interview he was very careful to say they were only theories, albeit theories based on knowledge gained when he worked for British intelligence. Nothing has ever been proved.

Richard Tomlinson made headlines in New Zealand — but he was still being gagged.

The mystery of Richard Tomlinson will not go away. At the time I met him in Nice, he was under the watchful eye of French intelligence. France and the UK are allies — the UK had issued a warrant for his arrest. Why did the French, who had mistreated him in the past, not simply arrest him and ship him back to London? Was he helping the French? Tomlinson denied it. He was vague about his sources of income, the money for a villa he had in the hills, and a 33-foot yacht in the harbour, which he had called *Aotearoa*, the Māori name for New Zealand.

Tomlinson eventually received an apology from the British government and was allowed to return to live in the UK without fear of prosecution, provided he refrained from talking to journalists about his time in MI6 and did not attempt to write any more books. The deal strongly indicated that he had not released the infamous list of agents.

No intelligence agency would ever forgive the exposure of its officers. Employees of MI6, MI5 and GCHQ are now able to take claims of unfair dismissal to industrial tribunals, a victory of sorts for Tomlinson.

He has retrained as a pilot. But it has proved difficult to find work in Britain or Europe, despite his skills. He is effectively exiled in Africa, where he has been working alongside the Nigerian Air Force, flying missions over parts of the country controlled by the Islamist group Boko Haram. But he still appears to be offside with western intelligence services. When Nigeria took delivery of several Diamond DA42 Twin Star aircraft registered in America, pilots flying the planes, which are fitted with sophisticated cameras, were required by the US Federal Aviation Administration to complete a training course either in the US or in Switzerland. Tomlinson applied for the training course, but received a letter from US authorities to the effect they would not allow him to join the course because, the Transport Security Administration explained, 'The TSA is unable to determine that you do not pose a threat to aviation or national security.'

■ ■ ■

Tomlinson was a threat only because he talked to journalists. Targeting the messenger as well as the message is a favourite truth-suppression tool. It's frequently used against those who are powerless to fight back — such as ordinary men and women trying to protect their country's rainforest …

2.

From the toolbox:
Shoot the messengers

IF A FOREST IS DESTROYED AND NO ONE IS THERE TO SEE IT, DOES ANYONE CARE?

IN THE NEWS, 18 JUNE 1989

Honey I Shrunk the Kids **tops box office**
John Wayne Bobbitt gets married
Tories in turmoil turn on Thatcher
    after election flop
'Green BP' accused of destroying rainforest

The guards were carrying pistols and clubs and they looked ready to use them. They were barking out questions to the forestry service official that stood in front of them. What do you want? What are you doing here? Who are your companions? I was standing a few feet behind the man from the forestry service and the guards kept looking in my direction. One of them had his hand on his gun. We were at the entrance to a mine on a remote road in Jamari National Forest in the state of Rondonia, in the Amazon. I was sweating profusely and my mouth was dry. An argument broke out as the questioning continued. The lead guard was waving his arms about, as was the forestry official.

During my weeks in Brazil, I had grown to love the sound of the Portuguese language, even though I could not speak it. It conjured up images of samba music and pretty girls on beaches but now it sounded harsh and threatening. In the distance I spotted a guard who appeared to be carrying a Kalashnikov rifle. I tried to edge my way back towards the car we had driven up the twisty, dusty road. My plan was to open the back door and sit in the car, out of the firing line if only temporarily.

At all costs I had to avoid answering any questions as my Portuguese was limited to ordering beer and *feijoada*, a black bean stew. It would have taken just seconds for the guards to realize I was not a forestry service official, despite being dressed like one. My cover story would be blown and if they searched me they would discover I had hidden a small camera and a notebook. I started thinking how easy it would be to make someone disappear in this vast wilderness on what could be my final assignment.

The London-based Insight team of *The Sunday Times,* of which I was a member, were investigating the destruction of the world's rainforests for minerals and timber and the involvement of governments and corporations in this activity. We had been tipped off that BP, one of the world's biggest oil companies, owned a mining operation that was damaging part of the Amazon rainforest. But we did not know the name of the subsidiary company, or where it was based, or where the mine was.

The Amazon rainforest covers nearly 7 million square kilometres (2.7 million square miles), which is about the size of the United States minus Alaska and Hawaii; it is nearly the size of Australia and bigger than the European Union. Finding a needle in a haystack might be simpler. Dozens of phone calls to Brazil followed but most of the people said they knew nothing or did not want to help. We were calling government officials, non-government organizations or NGOs, fellow journalists in what was largely a fishing expedition and I wasn't catching any fish. This is the unglamorous but very necessary part of investigative reporting.

Finally, I found someone prepared to help. I flew to the sprawling city of São Paulo, the largest in Brazil which has a modern financial centre surrounded by third-world slums. Tourists can visit a neo-Gothic cathedral and modernist architect Oscar Niemeyer's curvy Edifício Copan, a 38-storey residential building. The colonial Pátio do Colégio church marked the spot where Jesuit priests founded the city. I went to the offices of the Instituto de Antropologia e Meio Ambiente (IAMA), an NGO that investigated anthropological and environmental issues, where I met Mauro Leonel, an environmentalist and sometime journalist.

He was determined to bring to public attention the damage done to indigenous populations from roads built through the rainforests. These roads, developed to exploit mineral and timber resources, he said, had disregarded the social and territorial rights of the local people. He added how they also brought 'the massive, unnecessary and ridiculous destruction of entire ecosystems which will be forever lost'. One of the areas he studied was in the state of Rondonia, in the northwest of the country:

First the Indians were slowly expelled from the large rivers. The Spanish and Portuguese colonizers have used the rivers to extract minerals since the seventeenth century, therefore the Indians lost the sides of these rivers, which were transformed and made valuable as routes of fluvial commerce. At the end of the last century, came the rubber latex extraction and the Indians were again pushed away, from the smaller rivers, to their sources, and then came the dispute for the tributaries. However, none of these facts have been as fatal to the Indians as the building of roads.[1]

There had been a long list of atrocities from 'Punitive expeditions organized by gold miners, mining companies, rubber extraction, cattle and agriculture companies. The most notorious of these massacres took place in 1961 at Parallel 11, when the Cinta-Larga village was bombarded by an airplane ... Later the survivors were killed with terrible cruelty.'

Rondonia was a major source of cassiterite, the ore used to produce tin, and its increased value led to an expansion in construction and mining. Mauro said big companies had determined the region's public policies for decades. We knew the BP operation was mining for tin and Rondonia seemed like a good place to start. I went to Porto Velho, the state capital of Rondonia, 2465 kilometres (1532 miles) away, which involved three plane rides and a day's travelling. I hired a car and drove to Ariquemes. I had studied the scientific importance of the rainforest but being in it was another matter. For a start, Ariquemes seemed to be the mosquito capital of the world with giant insects, heat and humidity. It was not my idea of a holiday destination.

For days I was holed up in a small hotel in Porto Velho, living off bean stew and cold beer, waiting to meet officials from the forestry service. Mauro had made contact with a group of them. They knew which mines were causing damage and their job was to protect the forest. Local people warned me that the forestry service was often prevented from investigating the mines — the mining companies had the money, and political power, and they had guards and guns.

I was finally able to confirm that the Santa Barbara mine, in the Jamari National Forest, was owned by a subsidiary of BP. A group of forestry service men agreed to take me there. They would try to talk their way past the guards and into the mine. Our cover story was that it was an official inspection. I was dressed up as a forestry service worker — a uniform similar to a Scout's. I would go in with a group and hope nobody tried to talk to me.

Outside the mine, I was convinced our bluff had failed. I had managed to get back into the car and sat there for several minutes, trying to look calm and inconspicuous. I had to concentrate hard on my breathing. The argument raged on in front of me and voices were raised. But then I noticed a sudden change in mood. Cigarettes were offered to the guards, there was laughter and an animated but obviously friendlier discussion broke out.

After a few minutes, the guards shook hands with the forestry men. They returned to their concrete gatehouse, my colleagues got back into the car and we drove into the mine. The forestry service men had simply changed the subject and engaged the guards in discussing the great Brazilian passion for football. The guards were bored; they did not have many visitors and were happy to argue about favourite teams and players. They forgot all about me.

Inside the security cordon of the Santa Barbara mine, I was astonished by the view. Verdant Amazonian rainforest was rapidly being transformed into a moonscape of cratered, opencast mines.

Signs of dying forest were everywhere, with some trees felled, others shrivelling under thick coatings of dust. At the main site a huge area of previously untouched forest had been cleared, all vegetation and soil churned up and shifted by giant earthmoving equipment. Holes up to 30 metres (100 feet) deep had been dug and the earth was scarred, cracked and dry.

Clumps of burnt Brazil nut trees — protected under Brazilian law — stood silhouetted against the arid land. Abandoned mining sites in the Santa Barbara were bare even years after they had ceased to be worked. Not even scrub grew, and no attempt had been made to repair the damage by replacing topsoil and replanting. The destruction extended beyond the new sites being mined. Large amounts of soil were being dumped haphazardly, silting up one of the main rivers in the forest. The forestry service official was in despair. He had no real powers to inspect the site he was trying to protect — he could only watch as the rainforest was destroyed. 'This is not a national forest, it's a national disaster,' he said. The mine was so huge that only a small area could be watched over by the armed guards.

We managed to drive to a place away from prying eyes. I fetched the small camera that I had tucked away in the bottom of my shoulder bag and took a picture. There was a digging machine and truck in the foreground and forest in the far distance. But all else was bare and I easily imagined I was standing on the surface of the moon with no signs of life. There was no doubt that mining, road clearance, soil dumping and the diversion of rivers had caused the damage. On the way out I hid the camera in the boot of the car in case we were searched, but the guards just waved us through.

There was a bitter irony to what was happening to the forest. The devastation was being wrought by a British company which, 9600 kilometres (6000 miles) away in its London headquarters, had embarked on a multimillion-pound advertising campaign to convince its western customers that conservation was its creed. BP was going green.

On the 25th floor of Britannic House, the City of London headquarters of BP, an impressive line-up of six executives sat across the table from me. The group included senior management, public relations personnel, a lawyer and a geologist. The line-up seemed designed to intimidate, six against one. I had carefully prepared for the meeting, reviewing my notes and listing a series of questions based on what I had actually seen and interviews with local officials.

But their side of the table had stacks of documentation, consisting of reports, surveys and maps. It was one of the tactics used by large corporations faced with awkward questions. They always have better resources than any journalist, even one from a profitable newspaper like *The Sunday Times*. A giant corporation like BP could produce lots of officials and people with impressive sounding titles, and the studies they had commissioned, and other official-looking legal and scientific papers, with an alternative interpretation of the facts. Drowning you in documents, burying the truth beneath the paperwork, is a common corporate tactic. As I sat listening to their responses to our investigation, I couldn't help wondering where the wood in the impressive conference table came from.

The Insight investigation had revealed that leading retailers, including Marks & Spencer and Harrods, were selling tropical hardwood furniture. The stores admitted they did not know where the timber came from, or whether the forests were managed on a sustainable basis. We had even found that the reception rooms at Number 10 Downing Street were being refurbished using mahogany from the Amazon rainforests. The table looked like it was made of tropical hardwood. The *Sunday Times* investigation was a clear threat to the company's image.

BP was heavily promoting its environmental awareness with a £20 million rebranding campaign. It included painting its garages, tankers and ships predominately green with advertising slogans such as 'now we're greener than ever' and 'for all our tomorrows'. BP had invested in environmental protection work in North America and Europe, where legislation and public opinion prevented the kind of destruction that was going on in the Amazon. The company produced a document called 'A climate of progress: why sound environmental management is essential for sustainable growth'.

'BP aims for excellence in environmental matters,' it read. 'BP's operating companies worldwide recognise that the pursuit of environmental excellence is a necessary condition for business success. Society is entitled to demand that the right balance between conservation and economic development should be found. You can be sure that BP will always strive to achieve that balance wherever we operate.'

The document said that the regulatory environment was somewhat less structured in Latin America than it was in North America but BP aimed to apply the same environmental process wherever possible. Faced with the evidence I had gathered at the Santa Barbara mine, BP admitted that its work in the Amazon was not perfect.

Exactly how much rainforest had been destroyed was disputed, as monitoring land use in the wilds of the Amazon was not an exact science. The mining company later said the total directly cleared for opencast mining was 5400 hectares (13,500 acres), still an area the size of the British city of Southampton. But a survey commissioned by the World Bank estimated that only 60 per cent of the Jamari National

Forest had been left untouched by the mining operation. The remaining 40 per cent — the damaged area — amounted to 88,000 hectares (220,000 acres) of rainforest.

The executives at headquarters, when questioned about whether the balance between commerce and conservation was being achieved in their mining operation, replied, 'You're talking of the social cost benefit and we're a private company [in Brazil]'. They defended the operations of its security force in the Amazon: 'Our security people, with the appreciation of state forestry authorities, police the whole area. Security men are not known for being nice. It's a tough business we're in.' BP said that, 'the area is first and foremost a mining area which is held under mining rights from the department of mines'.

The company's argument was that it held the legal rights to exploit the area two years before the protected forest was established. Its argument amounted to this: we were there first and it is up to the Brazilian government to sort out any conflicts. The company knew that it could make that argument and win because Brazil at the time was a country of powerful mining interests and weak environmental protections.

The country had been run by a military regime from 1964 to 1985, and the 1980s became known in Brazil as the lost decade. The decade began with huge strikes around São Paulo. Workers were complaining about low wages and their leaders were arrested under national security laws. Brazil had to borrow money from the International Monetary Fund, which imposed an austerity program.

The military leaders were frequently at odds with the powerful Roman Catholic Church over the issue of land reform. At one stage the government expelled all foreign priests — many of them activists leading campaigns for reform. Expanding petroleum production and exploitation of natural resources through mining were used to offset the country's huge debts. In 1984, public demonstrations in major cities all over Brazil challenged military rule, which ended in 1985.

In October 1988, the National Constituent Assembly restored civil and public rights such as freedom of speech, independent prosecutors (Ministério Público), direct and free elections and a universal health system. It also decentralized government, empowering local and state governments. But the changes left intact the power of the old Brazilian landowners and the mining companies. In the aftermath of my story, the old guard went on the offensive. But they chose not to attack me, or the powerful media company that I represented. Instead they went after the people who had helped me.

■ ■ ■

A letter from Mauro Leonel arrived two months after the story was published. I had spent time basking in my journalistic scoop, taken a few days off and then had moved on to our next investigation. The letter was a reminder that serious journalism has consequences — that it is never just a story. The journalist leaves but life goes on for those you leave behind.

The letter was on IAMA notepaper.

It was a bizarre and sinister turn of events. Forestry service officials who had been doing their best to protect the rainforest from damage were being accused of incompetence by the Brazilian government's

IAMA' – Instituto de Antropologia e Meio Ambient

The Institute of Anthropology and the Environment
a non-profit non-governmental institution

Rua Turi, 16 / Sao Paulo, SP / 05443 Brazil

Tel. (55.11) 210.1338 - 210.1301

Fax. (55.11) 257.6455

Mr. Stephen Davis
The Sunday Times
1 Pennington Street
London E1 9XW
England

São Paulo, August 21, 1989.

Dear Stephen,

Thank you for your letter and for the refund of my
expenses. Unfortunately I have inform you that IBAMA
officials in Brasilia have accused the Rondonian officials
of negligence with respect to the damage caused BP in
Jamari. The truth is that the Rondonian officials were
interested in solving the problem, as you had the
opportunity to see in our visit to the area. In face of
these facts, I am asking you the favour to write a letter to
the President of IBAMA, Dr. Fernando Cesar Mesquita,
clearing the question. We from IAMA would like to have a
copy of this letter so that we may inform the Rondonian
officials that we are doing our best to exempt them from
these unjust charges.

My personal observations are that the local officials
had great disposition and competence to deal with the
problem of BP in the Jamari National Forest, specially
because of the excellent action of their director, Mr. Luis
Alberto Cantanhede. I am writing you this letter aiming to
prevent whatever misunderstanding that may arise with the
series of articles published by the Sunday Times. I thank
you very much for this additional favour.

Sincerely yours,

Mauro Leonel

environmental agency — confusingly named IBAMA, the Brazilian Institute of Environment and Renewable Natural Resources. Rather than investigate the mining company, they were going after the people who helped expose the operations of the mine.

It is one of the most popular truth-suppression tactics, deployed many times in many countries. Western media companies will generally defend their journalists and their stories, and deploy political, legal and financial resources to do so, although I fear that in the future, limited resources for serious journalism will make it less likely they will be up for a fight. But sources on the ground do not have that level of support. In this case, the jobs of the forestry service workers were under threat.

The story generated headlines and a burst of interest in the rainforest but *The Sunday Times* was unable to stop the forestry service officials being disciplined and their careers derailed. When we attempted to track them down later, no one would talk to us and the mining operation carried on. Governments and corporations know that if they just wait long enough, the media will move on to the next big story. In the years after our groundbreaking investigation, the destruction of the rainforest became a major story — a regular feature of media investigations. But we live in the age of the short attention span, and reporters travel less. Very few media organizations today would fund a long and expensive trip to Brazil looking for a needle in a haystack.

The investigative reporting is less frequent but all these years later the rainforest is still under threat. In Rondonia and other states mining is now more regulated and western customers are more likely to pay attention to the sources of wood. But in Brazil the local market for hardwood, much of it illegally harvested, is stronger than ever. Deforestation in Brazil is on the rise again, after many years of decline. Recent studies show a rise of 30 per cent in a 12-month period, an all-time record. Between July 2015 and August 2016, about 4800 square kilometres (3000 square miles) were burnt so that cattle could be grazed. Brazil is the world's top exporter of meat products.

In 2018, Brazil's supreme court upheld a new law that reduced some of the protections for the rainforest, enabling landowners to reduce the percentage of their land they must keep forested. The law also allowed them to cultivate land closer to hilltops and streams, areas particularly subject to erosion. The Amazon rainforest is still the lung of the planet and home to millions of rare species of plants, birds and insects. It is still vital to our future but it is now an old story. We have moved on. Our love of the new is an important part of the toolkit of deception. Old stories are boring and who has time to follow all the facts?

Even when a ship has sunk, drowning hundreds of people ...

3. From the toolbox: Our conspiracy theories are better than yours

THE ESTONIA MYSTERY: SPIES, SMUGGLERS, SECRET PACKAGES AND PUTIN

IN THE NEWS, 27 SEPTEMBER 1994

Call for Bosnian Muslims to have arms
Paul Newman donates $200,000
    to Rwandan aid
First day of jury selection in O.J. Simpson trial
Estonia ferry, 515 ft long passenger vessel,
    represents pride of a nation newly
    independent from the former Soviet Union

Tallinn, Estonia, 27 September 1994

The whistle blew, signalling the departure of the ferry *Estonia* and most of the passengers made their way to the outer deck to see it slip its moorings and back out into the harbour, stern first. The deck was crowded with happy people, waving and cheering as the ship left port, many of them red-faced Swedes who appeared to have consumed too much Aquavit, the potent local liquor.

It was 7 p.m., local time. The luxury ferry, its white hull reflecting the moonlight and its large superstructure glowing with lights, headed out into the Gulf of Finland. Beyond that, the formidable Baltic Sea and a 17-hour crossing to Stockholm. One of those on board was a man on a mission. His name was Avo Piht. The 39-year-old was a proud Estonian, a graduate of the Tallinn Maritime School and a former member of the Order of the Red Banner ferry company. He had spent nineteen years at sea and was happy to be on board the pride of the nation, the ferry named after the country, even though officially he was just there for the ride. Piht was on his way to Sweden for a test. If he passed, it would qualify him to sail into Sweden's capital without having to take on a local pilot.

When the ferry departed, there were two captains on board: Piht and Arvo Andresson, the captain on the bridge. Among the passengers were more than 500 Swedes. They included 60 officers from the Stockholm police department returning from a conference, a group of judges and members of a senior citizens club from Norrköping, who had paid $US120 each for a three-day shopping and sightseeing trip to Tallinn. There were 21 evangelists from the Jönköping church Pentecostal bible school. The other passengers came from Estonia, Latvia, Lithuania, Canada, Russia, Nigeria, Finland, Norway, Britain and Belarus.

Shortly after the *Estonia*'s departure, Captain Andresson made two announcements: they would reach the open sea in about three hours and when they got there, the weather would be bad. It had been cold and blustery when they left Tallinn. Soon that would turn into 6-metre (20-foot) waves and 80-kilometre (50-mile) per hour winds. Many of the passengers left the main lounge and headed back to their cabins. Some went via the outer deck, to look at the night sky and the sea. But not for long. The ship's lights were already picking out the white caps of the waves and the wind cut right through parkas and coats. A few of the passengers paused to look down into the blackness of the Baltic, and briefly wondered how cold the water was.

Seaman Silvie Linde had the midnight-to-8 a.m. watch and he began as usual with a tour of the car deck. The large open area was the most vulnerable part of the ship. Marine engineers, who had campaigned against the design of roll-on, roll-off ferries, regarded the deck as a fundamental flaw that rendered the ferries unseaworthy. Any leak or breach of the bow door would cause sea water to flood onto the deck and run the full length of the ship, which could rapidly cause the ferry to capsize and sink.

Since the *Herald of Free Enterprise* capsized as it left Zeebrugge in Belgium in 1987, there had been changes: installing video cameras for the bow doors so they could be seen on the bridge, and improved reporting systems, such as the visual structural integrity check seaman Linde was in the course of making. But ferry owners had resisted dividing the car decks with watertight bulkheads because it would reduce the number of cars on board and thus lower revenue. There would also be inconvenience for the passengers.

As seaman Linde crossed the car deck, he had trouble keeping his feet in the rough seas. But the deck was not as crowded as usual

— only 77 vehicles in a space that could take 400 — and there were no passengers as they were barred from the car deck while the ship was in open waters. Linde quickly reached the bow door and he carefully checked the huge metal hinges that held the door closed and confirmed that all was well. He was standing only a metre or so from the ramp that was lowered to let vehicles on and off and as he turned to leave he heard a loud bang. It seemed to come from the starboard side, underneath the bow door. He radioed the bridge and was told to remain on the car deck to look for signs of damage. He examined the whole area again, using his flashlight, but there were no other sounds or signs of a breach and after a few minutes he continued on his rounds. It was 12.40 a.m.

■ ■ ■

As usual, the casino was proving the most popular spot on the ship and the punters queued at the information kiosk to exchange cash for betting chips. A businessman was collecting a large sum of Swedish krona when the ship started rolling to starboard. The attendant was able to grab hold of the desk and steady herself but the money and chips were hurled on to the floor, along with the businessman who was saved from injury by the booze that had relaxed his muscles. As the man was helped to his feet, an officer rushed by and ordered that the kiosk be shut down for the night.

On the bridge the first mate checked the monitors as the crew fought to control the starboard roll, the *Estonia* tilting as it was hit broadside by a series of large waves. He could see water pouring into the car deck and shouted to the captain, 'The bow is breached, sir, the bow is breached.' The captain ordered the pumps to be switched on and reduced the speed of the ferry to 10 knots. He broadcast the code word for an emergency crew alert over the public address system: 'Mr Skylight. Repeat, Mr Skylight.' He then noted the time, 1.20 a.m.

Seaman Linde was on the foredeck when he heard the alert. When he tried to head back to his position, he met passengers coming up the other way. Some were shouting that there was water coming into the cabins on the first deck. He radioed the bridge: 'Water reported on deck one.' As he spoke, he felt the *Estonia* again begin to tilt to starboard. At 1.24 a.m. the captain ordered the radio room to broadcast a mayday. The message was picked up by another ferry, the *Silja Europa*.

> *Estonia*: 'Mayday, mayday.'
> *Silja Europa*: '*Estonia*, what's going on? Can you reply?'
> *Estonia*: 'We have problems here now, a bad list to the right side.
>   I believe its 20–30 degrees. Could you come to our
>   assistance?'
> *Silja Europa*: 'Can you give your position?'
> *Estonia*: 'We have a blackout. We can't get it now. I can't say.'

As the ship heeled, the lights went out. The emergency light came on for four to five minutes. Then it was completely dark. When the ship's funnel reached the water, witnesses could hear the bridge windows breaking. They also heard a long drawn-out typhoon signal. They saw the firing of a distress rocket. At this angle, diesel oil started to flow over the ship, making the surfaces slippery and treacherous. On the lower decks, most of the passengers had been asleep in their cabins and woke as their baggage toppled to the floor. In a few of the cabins, suitcases had crashed against the doors, preventing them from being opened.

Ice-cold water began to seep under the doors. Most of the passengers trapped in their cabins drowned as the ferry sank. A group of elderly passengers trying to make it to the lifeboats were met on the stairs by rushing water. Realizing all was lost, some got to their knees and began to pray. Others just stood where they were and wept. Most of those who made it to boat stations found there was no time to launch a life raft. As the *Estonia* began to slip beneath the waves, many leapt into the water. The temperature was below zero. Average survival time in the water was approximately four minutes. Stronger swimmers, fit and determined, lasted a bit longer. It was up to six minutes before their bodies were paralyzed by the cold and they lost consciousness and drowned.

At 1.27 a.m., the *Silja Europa* received a second mayday from the *Estonia*, saying things were very bad. *Silja Europa* replied, asking for the *Estonia*'s position again and again. But there was only silence. Three things had happened very quickly, dooming the *Estonia*. A torrent of water had rushed into the communications room, knocking out the radio and radar. In less than two minutes, the ferry had tipped over on its starboard side, submerging the bridge beneath the waterline, and the huge volume of water sloshing through the car deck began dragging the ship down. And the impact of the waves had battered open the 55-tonne visor that protected the bow, leaving it open to the stormy seas.

■ ■ ■

Paul Barney was certain he was about to die engulfed by the black, cold ferment of the Baltic Sea. He no longer felt cold. He had stopped shivering and was ready to let go. Death seemed like a warm, comfortable place to be and it was all around him. Hundreds of bodies floated in the water. The *Estonia*, where he had been sleeping hours earlier, had disappeared beneath 75 metres (250 feet) of water. *What an incredible waste*, the British geologist and landscape architect thought. *I'm only 35. I haven't lived long enough.* Then he got angry: *I want to live. I want to go on with my life.*

Barney, from Pangbourne, Berkshire, was returning from a study trip. He had been sleeping on a bench in the Café Neptune, near the stern. At the last moment he had decided against taking a cabin on one of the lower decks. He was woken by a loud bang. He saw furniture was moving as the ferry started to list. Barney noticed his hand was cut and bleeding but he had no time to think about how it had happened. He found himself clinging to a doorframe with an Estonian man as the ferry tilted towards the icy Baltic waters.

Barney could see the blackness of the sea below, what looked like a ravine of water as the ferry turned on its side. Both men saw a lifebelt on a bulkhead nearby. Barney was wondering whether to go for it when the Estonian jumped towards it. But just at that moment a wave hit and washed him away. Barney never saw him again. Then the lights went out. Suddenly, the moon came out from behind the clouds and lit up pipework that had been on the ceiling of the promenade deck. The ceiling was now a wall. 'I just said, right, there's only one thing to do, climb that. So I climbed up and suddenly, there I was on top of this enormous ship, on my own, in my socks, and a massive gale and the waves breaking over the ship.'[1]

He found a small group of passengers desperately trying to board a life raft at the other end of the hull. He walked down the hull, terrified he would drop into a black hole, and reached the life raft just as it was being launched. 'I jumped in at the last moment as we hit the water, and immediately a wave turned the whole life raft upside down. So suddenly, I was upside down in the life raft in the pitch black. And I had to swim out. I came up to the surface, where everyone was around, sort of shouting and screaming. I was shouting for a life jacket.'

There were sixteen people on the life raft and they watched as the *Estonia* sank. Another passenger, who Barney quickly nicknamed Mr Positive for his upbeat comments, pointed at the sinking ship and said, 'Isn't it beautiful?' And it was strangely beautiful, Barney thought, the *Estonia* going down in a red smoky haze as the moon lit the scene. Like the famous pictures of the *Titanic* or a scene from a movie.

The next five hours were a grim battle for survival. Barney and the others had two options to choose from. They could sit or crouch in the icy water that had gathered on the upturned raft — it was like sitting in a paddling pool — and suffer hypothermia, or stand up to get out of the water, exposing themselves to the bitter wind, and hypothermia. They could see rescue helicopters above them and they waved and shouted but the pilots could not see them. They were bobbing around in the black water. At one stage, Barney was swept overboard by a wave but he managed to grab a piece of rope and cling on for dear life. When the sun came up, only six of the sixteen on the raft were still alive. Mr Positive was dead. Barney was the last one off the raft when a Swedish search and rescue helicopter finally found them.

At dawn, there were pyjama-clad corpses floating in the sea. A few life jackets were tossed back and forth by the waves. But of the *Estonia* there was no sign, no oil slick or collection of debris to mark the spot. As the sun rose over the Baltic on 28 September, the 15,600-tonne ferry had disappeared.

When the final count was made, 852 passengers and crew had lost their lives. In addition to 501 Swedes, the dead included 285 Estonians, seventeen Latvians, ten Finns and 44 people of other nationalities: one from each of Belarus, Canada, France, the Netherlands, Nigeria, Ukraine and the United Kingdom, two from Morocco, three from Lithuania, five from Denmark, six from Norway, ten from Germany and eleven from Russia.

The survivors of the shipwreck were mostly young, of strong constitution and male. Seven people over 55 years of age survived; there were no survivors under age twelve. About 650 people were still inside the ship when it sank. The rest were assumed to have reached the outer decks, where 160 of them boarded the life rafts.

A commission of inquiry was announced and the Swedish government assured its people that the ship would be raised from its grave and the bodies recovered. The governments of Sweden, Finland and Estonia made a joint, solemn public promise to their citizens and more especially to the families of the victims: no stone would be left unturned, no avenue unexplored to find the cause of the tragedy. But that's not what happened. Instead, the *Estonia* sinking has become a textbook example of truth prevention, which started just after the disaster and which continues to this day. It has involved several governments, intelligence agencies and an impressive array of conspiracy theories.

■ ■ ■

Avo Piht, sea captain, officially died on 28 September 1994, when the roll-on, roll-off car and passenger ferry *Estonia* sank in a storm in the Baltic Sea. He was the captain who went down with his ship. Captain Piht was listed among the long columns of dead in the official report commissioned by the Swedish and Estonian governments, which had only been completed and made public four years after what had been one of the worst maritime disasters in Europe since 1945. The verdict was that design faults and incompetent crew work were the causes of the tragedy.

But the initial paperwork compiled in the immediate aftermath of the disaster, the interviews with survivors and the logs of the helicopter crews who had lifted them from the freezing water all tell a different story. Piht had originally been listed among the survivors — and to appear on the list you had to give your full name, date of birth and nationality. An elderly German woman said she saw a man she later identified as Piht in a life raft after the *Estonia* had gone down. The helicopter mission log, with an attached statement from the loadmaster, said that 24 people had been taken from that life raft to the Finnish island of Utö. Twenty-four people landed at Utö, according to the crew, but only 23 arrivals were later recorded in the findings of the international commission of inquiry.

There were also stills taken from a Swedish freelance video cameraman's shots of surviving passengers being treated at a clinic in Turku, with one shot showing a man moving quickly through the back of the crowd, a man who bore more than a passing resemblance to Captain Piht. Lots of people looked for Piht in the aftermath of the disaster; some are still looking. The survivors, and the families of the dead, have never given up the quest. There have been wild rumours and conspiracy theories and the occasional 'sighting', but every one of them has turned out to be a false alarm or an invention by some publicity-seeking nutcase.

■ ■ ■

Outside Scandinavia, the *Estonia* story reports attracted little publicity after the initial news. I am a news addict but I had only a vague memory of the story when I was approached by an intelligence source — an MI6 officer who had worked on the Russia desk — who suggested I investigate what had happened to the *Estonia*. He suggested that the sinking of the *Estonia* was not an accident and that Britain, Sweden and the Baltic nations had good reason to want the truth to stay buried. The country of Estonia had been used, he said, as a transit point to get sensitive military technology out of Russia and on to ferries heading for the West.

When I began my investigation, it was clear there was a lot we did not know. The *Estonia* had capsized and sunk in less than 45 minutes, an extraordinarily fast time — faster than ships that had been sunk by collisions or torpedoes. It had gone to the bottom in 75 metres (250 feet) of water, 32 kilometres (20 miles) south of the coast of Finland, at 1.48 a.m.

A model of the Estonia.

It was equally clear that the promises of transparency in the investigation had been abandoned. The Swedish government had reneged on its promise to raise the wreck and to spare no cost in finding the cause of the disaster. Sweden's leaders had changed their minds, refusing all pleas from the bereaved relatives to bring the *Estonia* to the surface, even though it lay in shallow waters and maritime engineers had said it would be a relatively easy salvage job.

Having agreed that there was a moral and legal case for salvage, so that the relatives could bury their dead and the cause of the disaster be clearly established, they now made the opposite case, that the ethical thing to do was to leave the 650 dead at the bottom of the sea. The promise to spare no expense to salvage the ferry became, just a few months later, a decision that it would be too costly. Instead of a salvage operation, they decided to bury the *Estonia* in a cement shell — a physical attempt at truth suppression.

An international consortium, led by Swedish building firm NCC, was hired to encase the ferry's wreck with three layers of textile, sand and a prefabricated cement mattress. The reason given was that it would fend off graveyard robbers and plunderers. Such a method required no divers. The project was supposed to take a year and all staff would receive special training for the macabre operation. 'The covering will provide ample security against intrusion. The stone formation will evoke thoughts of a burial mound,' the government explained. Relatives who had formed lobby groups to try to force Stockholm to bring home the bodies of their loved ones accused the government of heartlessness and of ignoring their wishes.

The attempt to seal the wreck failed and was later abandoned. The appearance of a cover-up, literally and metaphorically, was strengthened by the signing of the *Estonia Agreement 1995*, a treaty that sought to prevent any exploration of the wreck, even though it lay in international waters. The agreement, which many maritime law experts regard as legally dubious, was signed by Sweden, Finland, Estonia, Latvia, Denmark, Russia and, strangely enough, Britain. A glance at a map would show how odd this was. Britain is not a Baltic nation. It had no obvious connection to the Baltic or the disaster bar the fact that one Briton, John Manning, had died in the sinking and a second, Paul Barney, had survived. Other non-Baltic countries with passengers who had died on the ferry did not become signatories to the treaty. There was no precedent for Britain signing such a treaty. I made two requests under the Freedom of Information Act to the Foreign Office in London, for background and briefing papers on why Britain signed the Estonia Agreement, but never received a reply.

The disaster had not received the attention it deserved outside the Scandinavian and Baltic countries. The families of the victims kept up their campaign for answers but they needed help. It came from an unusual source — a slightly eccentric American named Gregg Bemis, whose claim to fame was that he owned one of the world's most famous shipwrecks, the *Lusitania*. That British ship was bound for Liverpool after a transatlantic crossing in 1915 when it was struck by a torpedo from a German submarine off the southeast coast of Ireland during World War I. It sank in just eighteen minutes. Of the 1962 passengers and crew aboard, 1198 died, most of them from drowning and hypothermia.

The attack prompted outrage: 128 Americans were killed in the disaster and that helped push the United States into World War I. The shipwreck now lies on its starboard side, at a depth of about 90 metres (300 feet) off the coast of County Cork. Bemis had been the sole owner of the wreck since 1982 when he bought it for US$1.

When I met Bemis, in London, he was frustrated with the apparent lack of interest in the *Estonia* disaster from the mainstream media in the West and by the efforts of the Swedish government to prevent him getting to the truth. Along with Jutta Rabe, a German TV producer, he had turned his considerable resources to sponsoring a diving operation that had gone down to the wreck. The expedition had gone ahead despite opposition from the governments of Sweden, Estonia and Finland, and harassment by the Swedish Navy; illegal harassment, since the wreck was in international waters.

The Swedes forced Bemis's diving operation to sail from neutral Germany rather than closer Sweden or Finland. This reduced the time his team could spend diving. The Swedes also despatched military speedboats to circle his ship while coastguard officers boarded and demanded a crew list. Despite this, seven divers from the expedition made trips down to the wreckage, filming video and bringing up pieces from the hull. They survived a near disaster when in stormy weather one of the divers was swept off the deck of the ship *One Eagle* and was rescued.

The *One Eagle* team found and filmed a hole near the bow and brought up pieces of metal cut from near the bow door. Tests of the metal at laboratories in the United States and Germany showed signs of an explosion on the ferry's hull. 'The results show changes to the metal similar to those seen by high-detonation velocity,' one report concluded. The Swedish government's response was not to re-open the investigation but to try to deploy that favoured tool: shoot the messengers. They issued arrest warrants. 'We have a law which makes the *Estonia* an inviolable grave site,' said Deputy Trade Minister Mona Sahlin, who had earlier written to Bemis asking him to call off the expedition.

'I have decided to arrest in their absence Bemis and Rabe as jointly responsible for the dive,' prosecutor Ronnie Jacobsson told Reuters. 'This means that if either of them sets foot in Sweden, we want to talk to them on suspicion of having violated the law protecting the *Estonia* grave site. For the moment it is not a question of seeking their extradition,' he added.

The US State Department warned Bemis to 'back off' his investigation, and to this day he faces arrest and possible imprisonment if he ever sets foot in Sweden. The groups representing the survivors and the relatives of the victims, however, were more interested in what had been found and the results of the tests. As Lennart Berglund, chairman of the Foundation of Estonia Victims and Relatives, said after Bemis's expedition: 'There's still a lot of evidence down there. Their major argument was that there was nothing new; now there is something new.' The Baltic nations, however, remained firm in saying there would be no new inquiry.

The Swedish government had hired their own diving team from Rockwater, a British-based division of the American Halliburton group, run between 1995 and 2000 by Dick Cheney, later US vice-president. Halliburton was long rumoured to have connections with the CIA. This team produced thirteen videotapes showing the wreck, they said, from every angle. But one angle was missing and some Swedish politicians later argued that the videos had been edited.

The authorities continued to insist there was no explosion. There had already been an inquiry set up. It had concluded in 1997, albeit after bitter disputes among its members, that faulty locks on the bow doors of the *Estonia* were the cause of the disaster, along with the crew's failure to react quickly enough to the crisis by reducing the ferry's speed. The 50-ton bow door, battered by high seas, had been ripped off as the locks gave way, letting water flood into the car deck, and the ferry had become unstable and overturned, the investigation concluded.

EXPERT TESTIMONY

Disasters in the modern era like *Estonia* and 9/11 are always followed by the appointment of commissions who take expert testimony and then produce reports. Sometimes these reports and their conclusions are challenged by other experts, who appear equally well qualified.

Reporters seldom have the depth of knowledge to challenge the expertise of engineers, scientists and others who always come with impressive-sounding qualifications.

How should journalists and their readers, listeners and viewers treat such reports when there are disputes?

In my experience, the majority of experts in these cases are conducting real experiments and espousing genuinely held beliefs based on a vast amount of knowledge and experience.

But it is true that the selection and use of expert testimony can be used to support or discredit a theory. Governments and corporations can easily emphasize information that supports their case, and downgrade or ignore details that don't.

In a plane crash for instance, the plane maker and the engine manufacturer will want to steer away from any questions of mechanical fault. The pilots' union will be hoping to avoid discussions of pilot error. If you are a national airline — the pride of your country — and your plane was deliberately crashed, you will be doing all you can to point the finger in another direction. Fault-finding is followed by battles over compensation. Who foots the bill when the grieving relatives sue?

The most important rule, though, is this: in every major disaster, there are gaps in the evidence, things which cannot be explained, inconsistencies and contradictions. These gaps are often exploited by conspiracy theorists, for whom the absence of evidence is evidence. But they are in the nature of the event itself.

Disasters are investigated after the event. The experts weren't there to record everything in detail as the plane crashed, the ship went down or the building collapsed. There may be eyewitnesses but their testimony is not always accurate. In fact, eyewitness testimony has been shown to be the least reliable form of evidence. When you are fighting for your life or looking at something truly horrific, your brain is not dispassionately recording everything you see.

Hence the gaps and the inconsistencies, and the fallibility of both expert and eyewitness testimony. We can't know everything about these disasters and tragedies and we never will.

The survivors of the *Estonia* and the relatives of the victims had been promised transparency but what they got were layers of secrecy. An Estonian parliament committee of investigation summed up the doubts of many: 'None of the investigations conducted to date has been sufficiently thorough. There has been no official examination of the cargo transported on board and on the vehicle deck of the ferry ...' The committee complained that the criminal investigation into the sinking had been conducted in great secrecy.

Marine engineers challenged the official inquiry's conclusions on technical grounds. Investigators from Meyer Werft, the German shipyard that built the *Estonia*, raised the possibility of an explosion; the lab tests done on the material that the Bemis expedition's divers brought to the surface also showed traces of a detonation, which could explain the loud bang heard by Linde and others on board the ferry on the night it went down.

Two other examinations of the metal also concluded that there had been an explosion. A hole in the hull was a much more likely explanation for the catastrophic demise of the *Estonia* and its rapid sinking. If an explosion sank the ferry, what kind of device was used and who had planted it? Who had the blood of 852 people on their hands? My inquiries pointed east, in the direction of Moscow.

Estonia, like the other Baltic nations Latvia and Lithuania, had been part of the Soviet Union but had achieved independence after its break-up. The new nations were proud of their new status and fiercely independent. But they were also home to substantial Russian-speaking minorities, and the new Russia, like the Soviet state, considered the Baltics to be within their sphere of influence. The Baltic nations became the centre of a battle for influence and information between competing intelligence services from Russia and the West. The Baltics were, in the memorable words of the writer, journalist and Russia expert Edward Lucas, like a sweet shop for spies — accessible, target rich and friendly.

It was a new cold war and at the centre of this particular battle was Estonia, a small country with a population of just over 1.3 million, most of whom live in the capital, Tallinn. There are plenty of direct air, road and rail connections between Moscow and Tallinn and by the early 1990s it had become a favourite smuggler's route from Russia to the West, for people, contraband and for weapons and technology. Once a package reached Estonia it was a simple ferry ride to Stockholm and connections beyond.

When the Soviet Union collapsed, the old structures that had sustained it crumbled away. Intelligence officers and scientists, temporarily freed from the constraints of party discipline and fear of retribution, and looking ahead to a future where the West was ascendant, rushed to the exits. The Cold War seemed to be over, the Soviets had lost, and those who had information of value, to sell or smooth their passage to the West, were looking to make deals. It was a buyers' market and for western intelligence agencies, in particular the CIA and MI6, it seemed like every day was Christmas and the presents kept arriving.

Vasili Mitrokhin, a senior archivist in the Russian intelligence services, was one of those bearing gifts. He had catalogued the secrets of the state. After he made contact with an MI6 officer, the British arranged to get him and his family out. Later an officer went back to Russia and retrieved a huge amount of material that Mitrokhin had copied from the archives and buried in the garden of his *dacha* on the outskirts of Moscow. It was a treasure trove, a secret history of the KGB. Others were offering more up-to-date secrets.

One of the key targets for the intelligence services of the West was Soviet science and in particular the Strategic Rocket Forces of the Russian Federation, a military branch of the Russian Armed Forces that controlled Russia's land-based intercontinental ballistic missiles (ICBMs). The Soviet Union was gone but Russia still had thousands of missiles aimed at the West. The CIA and MI6 wanted to determine how safe they were, to see if command and control procedures were still in place, and if such procedures were robust enough to prevent the launch of a rogue missile by a disaffected commander. In particular, they needed to know how dangerous the nuclear threat was, how accurate the missiles were and what their actual range and targeting capabilities were.

Getting hold of missile telemetry, the results of the monitoring of flight trials and ground tests, was a key goal for the CIA and MI6. The fruits of the decades-long Soviet space program were another key target — details of rocket fuel and flight capability, guidance systems, alloys, satellites and what, if any, programs the Soviets had to develop space-based weapons. Test results would be a goldmine and getting hold of components would be even better. These were available and they were being smuggled to the West, through a joint operation involving MI6, the Swedish intelligence service, MUST, and the new Estonian intelligence service formed in 1992.

The British had helped the Estonians set up their new spy service after the country became independent and the two services worked hand in hand thereafter, often alongside the Swedes. It was no surprise therefore when Lennart Henriksson, a former head of customs in Stockholm, in an interview with Sveriges Television, blew the whistle on a major intelligence smuggling operation.

The ferry *Estonia*, he said, had been used for smuggling stolen Russian military equipment to the West. The shipments had been let through on orders from 'the highest authorities'. He had personally witnessed two such shipments.[2] The comments caused uproar in Sweden and led to a fresh inquiry under Johan Hirschfeldt, president of the court of appeal. But once again there was a strange reluctance to look at new evidence. Despite a formal offer from Bemis, Hirschfeldt's investigation declined to look at the evidence from the private diving expedition. It did confirm, however, that military equipment had indeed been carried on the ferry. There had been shipments just before the tragedy, on both 14 and 20 September 1994, as witnessed by Henriksson, and it had been a government operation. But the judge concluded the equipment was electronic and it had no connection to the disaster.

Hirschfeldt added, 'There is no basis for me to assume that the defence authority of the defence procurement office [in Sweden] was trying to transport defence materiel on board *Estonia* when the ship sank.'[3] Of course, intelligence services are not answerable to Swedish judges, particularly in regard to secret operations that involve key relationships between spies in several countries.

I enlisted the support of a Russian in my investigation, being well aware that Russia is a dangerous country for journalists, one where you can be murdered or made to disappear for asking the wrong question about the wrong person or story. A month after the sinking of the *Estonia,* Dmitry Kholodov, a Russian journalist investigating links between Russian military figures and organized crime, was told by an anonymous caller to collect a briefcase from the 'left luggage' area of a Moscow train station. The briefcase, he was told, contained important evidence for his investigation. He collected the suitcase and brought it back to his office. When he opened it a bomb exploded, killing him instantly. For this and other reasons, my Russian colleague will remain anonymous.

The *Estonia* tragedy had been reported in Russia but had quickly given rise to a set of conspiracy theories, many of them bizarre. One television report claimed that the Russian-Estonian mafia had placed a limpet mine on the hull using a miniature submarine, to warn the shipping company that it should pay protection money. There was another story that involved Arab terrorists sinking the *Estonia* on orders from Russian intelligence officers. Yet another said there were space laser systems on board, stolen from Russia and en route to the West.

Some of these stories reflected the tendency of the Russian media to publish or broadcast wild or conspiratorial theories but they also had all the hallmarks of *dezinformatsiya* (disinformation) — a specialty of Russian intelligence services throughout the Cold War, where faked documents and lies were leaked to journalists to embarrass, confuse and influence political debate. This is Fake News in the real sense of the term — designed to deceive or to distract people from the real story — as opposed to the current Trump definition of fake news, a label given to genuine stories that make him or his administration look bad.

Where there is a major disaster, conspiracy theories flourish. Gaps or inconsistencies in official accounts are investigated by legitimate journalists and pursued by survivors and relatives of victims. Questions are asked which governments cannot or will not answer. Winston Churchill once said: 'In wartime, truth is so precious that she should always be attended by a bodyguard of lies.' How better to disguise an actual conspiracy than to surround it with invented conspiracies — and the more outlandish the better. Legitimate questions are lost among the noise generated by these wild theories — amplified and spread by the internet. It all blurs together in the public mind. Attention is diverted to other things and as the years pass, the truth seems further and further away. The Russians had very good reasons to produce disinformation about the sinking of the *Estonia*.

■ ■ ■

The flood of secrets and technology that flowed out of the Soviet Union after it collapsed attracted the attention of a group of senior KGB officers, true believers who mourned the demise of the empire. They wanted to preserve and protect the secrets of the state and became determined to shut down the pipelines sending information to the West. They were known as the Felix group. Russians newspapers reported that the group had formed to assassinate corrupt politicians whom they blamed for the disintegration of the Union of Soviet Socialist Republics, the USSR. They were blamed for the murder of Oleg Kantor, a banker, one of a number of Russian bankers killed in mysterious circumstances. The group was also said to be targeting KGB officers involved in drug smuggling and other organized crime.

A few months after the *Estonia* sinking, a Felix group report was sent to media organizations all over the world. It comprised dozens of pages, most of them devoted to linking Chechens to organized crime. Russia was fighting a brutal war in Chechnya at the time. Alongside the anti-Chechen propaganda were allegations about organized crime in Estonia and that Estonia was a transit hub for illicit weapons from Russia to Europe. It then gave a seemingly detailed account of what had happened to the *Estonia*. It claimed that the account was based on wiretapped conversations.

It said the *Estonia* had two illicit cargoes on board — heroin and cobalt. Cobalt can be a gamma ray source and highly radioactive. The Felix account said that the ferry captain was involved in drug trafficking. A rival gang tipped off customs officers who were waiting in Sweden to seize the shipment and arrest the captain. But someone alerted the *Estonia*. The captain was ordered to rid the cargo of cobalt. They tried to get rid of the illicit cargo via the bow door and accidentally sank the vessel. It was a classic piece of disinformation — explain the sinking in a way that directed attention away from the state to non-state actors, blackening the reputations of Estonians, sowing confusion but with a kernel of truth and a warning: we know you were stealing our weapons and smuggling them out on the ferry.

An investigation by the Estonian parliament concluded: 'The so-called classified Felix report which appeared in the press … is an intentionally misleading document based on erroneous data. In all probability this report on organized crime was produced by special services of a state unfriendly to Estonia.' Among the early members of the Felix group, according to my sources, was the future Russian leader Vladimir Putin, who at the time of the *Estonia* tragedy was part of Russia's effort to stop the trade in secrets.

Intelligence sources have confirmed that the *Estonia* was carrying crucial data — telemetry and components — from the Soviet space and missile programs. The divers hired by the Swedish government, whose work is still an official secret, searched cabins occupied by a Russian space technology dealer, Aleksandr Voronin, who owned a company in Tallinn and who, along with his brother in Moscow, was suspected of trading in weapons and technology. British intelligence was behind the smuggling operation, working with the Swedes.

Intelligence sources say the Russians learnt of the smuggling operation and tried to stop it. One possible source of the tip-off to the Russians was a man called Herman Simm. Simm was a senior Estonian official. He was the country's top police officer at the time of the sinking. Later he was part of the state secret protection department and one of the liaisons with NATO, where he handled classified information. In 1998, Simm was arrested and convicted as a Russian spy. He had been selling them NATO secrets for a decade.

The Russians found out about the smuggling. Multiple sources say the *Estonia* was sunk by a mine explosion. The most likely explanation is that a mine was placed by Russian operatives or people acting for the Russian government, a third party contracted for the purpose. The Russian mine was designed to prevent the *Estonia* from completing its journey, to damage it and force it back to port. The aim was to stop the specific shipment or the smuggling operation in general — and/or to issue a warning to western intelligence agencies. But the operation went wrong and the mine caused more damage than was intended, possibly because of the state of repair of the locks on the bow door. The ship sank and 852 people died. There will of course never be any official confirmation of Russian responsibility for the explosion. Putin's Russia is not a place where transparency rules.

Russian media have been investigating the story for years but journalists who tried to get to the bottom of it and who raised questions about the involvement of the Russian government, were warned by the authorities to back off. Russia, like Britain, signed the agreement that prevents divers from exploring the wreck of the ferry. Even in the land of the free, the United States, documents about the sinking have been kept secret. There are at least three files about the sinking of *Estonia* in the archives of the National Security Agency (NSA). 'The documents are classified because their disclosure could reasonably be expected to cause serious damage to the national security,' according to the NSA.

■ ■ ■

There has been no explanation why Captain Avo Piht had apparently been rescued and then disappeared. Avo Piht has not been seen since the day of the sinking. But his family are adamant that he is still alive. Piht was one of eight people in one of the life rafts who were seen by witnesses and recorded as rescued. None of them has been seen since. Piht's wife Sirje received a call just after the accident stating he had been rescued and was safe and well. Two close friends of Piht saw him on TV among the rescued. Captain Erich Moik, a long-time friend of the family, had studied together with Piht at the Maritime Academy in Leningrad. He had just arrived in Rostock to take over the

Mare Balticum and had watched the television news with his crew at the hotel. They had immediately recognized their former colleague.

Piht had been taken from the Finnish island of Utö, together with other castaways, to the emergency room at Turku University Hospital; he had stood in front of an ambulance. Another witness from Stockholm, Heinrich Tann, who knew Piht from his regular trips on the *Estonia* later swore an affidavit stating he had clearly seen Piht on TV, alive and well. It seems fantastical that ships' captains and other passengers should be made to disappear in the aftermath of a disaster.

Each year since the sinking has brought new theories. The disaster has been seized on by sinister elements on the internet — among them anti-Semites who have declared, without any logic, that the Israelis did it. Such prejudiced views are of course helpful in a cover-up. Legitimate journalists asking questions can be lumped in with the lunatic fringe. Fantastic and unlikely theories are useful for governments trying to keep secret blunders or deliberate acts that cost the lives of innocent people.

The British and Swedish governments were secretly using public transport to smuggle stolen Russian military equipment. The western intelligence agencies were taking a risk by using the *Estonia*, in effect turning the passengers on the ferry into a form of human shield. Britain, Russia and Sweden, who are the major signatories to the *Estonia* treaty, still want the truth about the disaster buried, like the ferry itself.

4. From the toolbox: Delay, delay, delay until everyone gets bored

A MURDER CONFESSION IS IGNORED

IN THE NEWS, 29 SEPTEMBER 2014

Controversy over price of iPhone 6
Swedish scientists reveal competition to slip
   Bob Dylan quotes into research papers
Asian stocks fall on Hong Kong
   democracy protests
Coroner delivers verdict on
   missing Sydney man

Richard Sajko had reached the end of his shift at Avis Car Rentals in Mascot, near Sydney's domestic airport. It was midnight and he was readying to go home after what had been a quiet night. As usual, Richard had brought a meal packed by his grandmother. He was a quiet but not unfriendly young man and was known to his colleagues as an honest hard worker and there was never any trouble when Richard was around.

Richard walked to the dimly lit car park where his pride and joy, a red Holden Commodore with a V8 engine, was parked. A colleague also on her way home saw him reach the car and noticed that someone was sitting in the passenger seat waiting for him. The car must have been unlocked. The co-worker could not identify the other person as the car was too far away but for some reason she felt alarmed. She delayed driving off, pretending to look for something in her own vehicle while keeping the Commodore in sight in her rear-view mirror. Richard had a conversation with whoever was inside and then got in. Things must be okay, she thought and as she drove away she saw the lights of Richard's car come on.

At about 12.40 a.m. on that Sunday, 40 minutes after Richard left work at Avis, a witness being dropped home in a taxi spotted the red Commodore. It had been abandoned in Edwin Street in Ashfield, near Richard's home and 9 kilometres (5½ miles) from his workplace in Mascot. The damaged car was parked across a driveway, blocking it and obstructing the road. Richard loved the car and he would not have left it there in such a state and whoever had been driving had abandoned it in a hurry as the driver's door was open.

There was no sign of Richard. It would be eleven days before the police got round to looking into the abandoned car and made the connection with Richard's disappearance. The work colleague's glimpse in the rear-view mirror as she drove away from the Avis office was the last time anyone saw Richard Sajko alive. It was now Sunday, 14 May 1995, Mother's Day. Richard was an only child and his mum, Rozi, would never have a Mother's Day again. The Sajko case was to drag on for more than two decades, a prime example of a much-used truth-suppression tool — delay, delay, delay until the story goes away.

Richard had a good friend he looked up to named Sam Testalamuta Jr, who liked to be known as Sammy Testa. Sam's father owned a string of car dealerships in the inner west of Sydney. Sam was everything Richard was not, a sharp dresser, flashy and confident. Weeks before his disappearance, Richard had been assisting his mate Sam on a few jobs including washing cars for pocket money. Sam asked Richard to accompany him to pick up a car and take it to another location. He didn't own the car, said Sam, but he had permission to move it. Sam and Richard collected the car and put it on the back of a truck. As they were driving across Sydney they were pulled over by police. The car was stolen and both men were arrested. Richard said he did not know the car had been stolen. He had nothing to hide and agreed to be interviewed by police.

The Testalamuta family was angry that Sam had been charged. According to Richard's family, he came under pressure from the Testalamuta family and their lawyer to change his testimony. They wanted to challenge the police facts and have the matter dismissed at the first hearing. Despite his friendship with Sam, Richard refused to change his story. But he was a worried man and according to his mother, Rozi, he told her he had been threatened by Sam, who had said: 'I'll kill you and blow up your car.' Rozi was so concerned she had arranged an appointment to see an independent solicitor on 16 May.

Richard never made the appointment. Police checked Richard's phone records and discovered that his mobile phone had been used during the early hours of that Sunday morning by another young man, Faleata 'John' Tuiletufuga, who was an associate of Sammy Testa Jr. Police executed a search warrant at Tuiletufuga's home but he had allegedly gone to Melbourne. Later, when questioned about the Melbourne trip, Tuiletufuga could not explain how he had got from Sydney to Melbourne, 877 kilometres (550 miles) away. He couldn't explain where he had stayed or what he had done there or how he had got back to Sydney. According to later police reports, John

Richard Sajko. Missing or murdered?

Tuiletufuga, the adopted son of an Assembly of God preacher who was active in state politics, was confronted by his parents, who were alarmed by the police questions and the search warrant.

Tuiletufuga confessed to his parents that he had shot Richard dead on a Sydney beach and buried his body nearby. They took him directly to Ashfield Police Station to confess to the murder. But it was late at night and the officer in charge of the Sajko inquiry, Detective Sergeant Frank Mennilli, was not on duty. The Tuiletufuga family insisted the detective be contacted by phone. Tuiletufuga's father explained the situation to Mennilli and advised him about his son, 'He's here to confess'. Frank Mennilli had a difficult missing persons case. Now apparently it was a murder — and he had a chance to clear the case, with a confession. It was the kind of breakthrough to make an experienced detective's day. But Mennilli did not rush to the police station. It was the weekend. He told them to come back in a few days when he was back on duty.

The Tuiletufuga family returned to the police station several days later where they finally met the detective. Unusually, Mennilli took a statement from John Tuiletufuga before taking him to the interview room. He then had him read his statement into the interview tapes. This time there was no confession. In the formal interview, John Tuiletufuga denied killing Richard Sajko and claimed to have 'made it up'. Mennilli decided not to formally interview Sammy Testalamuta Jr or his family in spite of being aware of the alleged threats and the upcoming court case over the stolen car, opting instead to take a basic witness statement from Sammy Testa. The family were well known to the police. They had underworld connections and were thought by police to be involved in converting stolen cars.

Sammy Testa admitted visiting Richard during his shift at Avis on the afternoon of Saturday, 13 May. He was accompanied by Guy DiBella. DiBella and his girlfriend at the time had been charged with importing narcotics into Australia and were connected to a well-known motorcycle gang. Both men denied having anything to do with Richard's disappearance.

Rozi Sajko has spent two decades hoping that somehow the police would find her son's body and prosecute the man or men responsible for his death. She is convinced he was murdered. She is equally convinced that the police investigation was flawed from the start. She gave a statement to Detective Mennilli, a statement in which she alerted police to the threats made against her son before he disappeared.

> I was in a lot of pain, a lot of grief … I knew that something was not right. It didn't feel right to me the way he was directing my statement by the questions he asked in regards to the statement. How he was trying to steer it a certain way, I wasn't happy with that either. Instead of letting me say things as I wanted to, he wouldn't let me. He actually interjected various things and he wanted me to focus on that.

Rozi felt the statement did not place sufficient gravity on the threats. It was the beginning of what would be a contentious relationship with Mennilli.

> All I was interested in [was] getting to know or finding out what happened. Where is Richard? Who did what? I rang on a daily basis for weeks on end to the point where Mennilli rang my ex-husband and said to him, 'Can you please ring your wife and tell her not to ring every day, we can't tell her any more than what we have.'
>
> When I rang, hardly ever would anyone pick up or talk with me, they'd say someone will ring you back, I hardly ever got any calls back. There were no answers for me. I mean all I wanted to find out is, is there any news? Have you been able to find out anything? What can you tell me? I never really got any answers, I suppose they didn't have any answers for me. But at the same time I really felt that my feelings and concerns were being dismissed.

> *I didn't trust him. I had this terrible feeling that he was trying to protect Sam. I said to Joe [Rozi's husband] soon after when I started dealing with him, 'Something is not right here, he's very hostile towards me.' I definitely felt he was not showing any empathy, no sympathy, he was not forthcoming with information. If I asked any question, I was told, 'Oh I can't reveal that it is part of the investigation.' There was never any information given to me and I just felt that something was not right.*[1]

Among the things Detective Mennilli failed to mention to Rozi was that a man had confessed to killing her son. She did not find out for another eighteen years. Delay has featured from investigation all the way to inquest into the disappearance of Richard Sajko. Such delays prevented the story getting the attention it deserved until most of the Sydney media lost interest. It took a group of journalism students to start a new investigation.

There were no charges brought in the death of Richard Sajko and he was placed on the missing persons register. Later, following a recommendation from the coroner that all missing persons cases be reviewed, a new investigation was ordered. But resources to manage the cold-case inquiry were restricted. The regional commander, now Assistant Commissioner Frank Mennilli, told the team that there was insufficient staff available. The new team asked Detective Mennilli who he thought had killed Richard Sajko. He responded that he thought his father had done it. No evidence was offered for this theory — none has ever been offered. One of the new investigating team found the comment 'inexplicable'.

Mennilli was asked to supply a statement for the brief being prepared for the coroner. The statement would outline his initial investigation. Several months later, when his statement was handed over, it was only one-and-a-half typed pages. One of the detectives reinvestigating the case said the brief statement was extraordinary, given the complexity of the investigation.

The cold-case investigation went nowhere and the media again lost interest in the story as it had become old news. This is an all too common feature of modern journalism, where too many people have become slaves to the news cycle that was once 24 hours but now can often be measured in social media seconds. In a media-saturated society many people become easily bored and constantly want new information. In the rush to click around the online sites, people often do not wait to carefully judge or assess what is being presented. For a lot of people, stories have to be fresh and exciting or they are deemed too dull to share. The pressure is on most journalists to give the public what they want, which is something all new, all the time.

That pressure, combined with the lack of resources for long-term investigations means that many stories are not followed to their conclusion. If some of the facts are known, then the story has been told and it's old. The unanswered questions remain just that. For organizations or individuals that want to avoid scrutiny, that prefer not to answer awkward questions, the ever-shortening news cycle is a boon. The more you can delay, the better. It's an excellent truth-suppression tactic — any awkward line of questioning can be dismissed as old news. There may be new information — new facts that have come to light as the years have gone by — but they can be characterized and then dismissed as not newsworthy, just a variation on what we already know. In this way, significant information that can change the narrative of a story is framed by the authorities as a rehash — and journalists go along with that.

That is what happened with the Sajko story. You've got questions about Richard Sajko? An inquest is going to deal with those. A man confessed to the murder? That's already been reported. Any new developments? We can't add to what has already been said, the file is still open, the investigation is 'ongoing'. Old news.

■ ■ ■

In July 2014, nearly twenty years after Richard disappeared, an inquest was finally opened into his death. His mother Rozi thought it would at last be a chance for the facts to be heard and in an open hearing. The coroner could a take a fresh view of the case. Witnesses would be giving evidence under oath. Some of the details about the day he disappeared were no longer clear, many years later: whether he had sat in his car for a while or stood outside it and whether there was someone with him in the car when he drove away.

But other things were still very clear to Ian Bourke, the counsel for the coroner, who in his opening statement pointed to several pieces of evidence that suggested foul play. 'The evidence gathered to date suggests that Richard is dead. There is evidence to conclude that Richard died and died in very suspicious circumstances,' Mr Bourke said. 'He was the subject of verbal threats,' Mr Bourke told the court.[2] Mr Sajko was scared that Samuel Testalamuta 'might kill him or blow up his car' over a missed payment for a mobile phone. The lawyer also noted that both Richard and Sammy were facing charges over the stolen car. 'There might have been some pressure exerted upon Richard to change his account' about the car, Mr Bourke said.

Rozi Sajko was the first witness to give evidence. She said her son Richard had told her about Testalamuta's threats and the pending court case over the stolen car. She had told Richard she would get him an independent lawyer instead of the lawyer Testalamuta had provided.

But Sam's mother gave evidence that her son and Richard were good friends and that Sammy would never hurt him. Penelope Wass, SC, representing the Sajko family, challenged her description of Sam's good nature and said he had completed a ten-year sentence for shooting a man who was going to be a witness against him in another case. She said that Testalamuta was 'more than capable' of shooting a man because he had done so in 2002 in similar circumstances.

'You certainly knew that your son is more than capable of doing that … to another human being,' Wass asked Mrs Testalamuta.

'No,' she replied.

'He's done it before, why wouldn't he do it again?' Wass asked. 'Is it possible that you don't really know what your son is capable of?'

'No,' she replied.

Sam, who had just been released from jail, did not give evidence at the inquest but provided a statement that said he would never hurt his good friend Richard. 'I have never had any reasons to do that because he's a nice person and I don't know who would want to hurt him,' he said.

A former prostitute had a different view of the friendship. She said Testalamuta was one of her 'minders' while she was a working girl. 'Sam would joke with Richard by taunting him about the way he drove and used to call him stupid,' her statement said. 'Sam would use Richard a lot by having him do things for him … he would just basically use Richard as a gofer.'

The inquest examined the quality of the police investigation and why police refused to hear the confession by John Tuiletufuga. The court was told by Joseph Tuiletufuga that his son had told him he had shot a man at Bondi on the night of Sajko's disappearance. Tuiletufuga said that when he took his son to the police station to tell them about what he considered to be a confession to Sajko's murder, he was told to come back later. 'They said Detective Mennilli was not working till Tuesday.' He said the duty officer allowed him to phone Mennilli, but the detective just said, 'Could you come back on Tuesday?'

On the Tuesday, he told the inquest, his son told Mennilli the whole thing was a joke. Frank Mennilli told the court he didn't believe anything John told him. He said he could not recollect getting a phone call from the family at the police station. Both Mr Bourke and Ms Wass challenged him on why the original confession was not followed up. 'All the suspicions were there,' Mennilli said. 'There was no direct evidence.' Speaking about Rozi Sajko he said, 'I wish I could give her some good news. This is still a live investigation in my mind.' He said the disappearance had broken his heart and that he had never given up on solving the case. The coroner heard that phone records showed calls were made to acquaintances of Tuiletufuga from Richard's phone after he had disappeared.

One of the police officers who reinvestigated the case, former Detective Senior Constable Natasha Fraser, said in a written statement: 'It is my opinion that Richard's knowledge of Testalamuta's family's operations and the pending court case and the potential for Richard to turn police informer to expose the illegal operations of the family business is the motive behind Richard's murder.'

Another police officer, Detective Senior Constable Mark Hamilton, who had been pursuing this case for six years, was in tears on the witness stand as he told the court there was still no trace of Richard, despite DNA tests on bodies found all over Australia. But when the family's lawyer attempted to question Hamilton in detail, police lawyers objected. The inquest was abruptly shut down. The inquest had generated some headlines but the media moved on. There was little follow-up. It was filed away, under the category 'old story'. As far as major media was concerned, the story ended with the inquest.

As part of their investigative reporting unit, my journalism students at Macleay College in Sydney and Melbourne had made their own inquiries using Freedom of Information Act requests but there was a limit to what they could do. Three months after the inquest, deputy state coroner Carmel Forbes issued her findings. She referred the case back to the unsolved homicide unit of the New South Wales Police for further investigation.

> *I am satisfied on balance that Richard is deceased. Given the circumstances under which he disappeared, and the unexplained abandonment of his car, I am satisfied he died on or about 14 May 1995 in suspicious circumstances. There is insufficient evidence, at this time, to determine the place, manner or cause of Richard's death.*

The coroner then criticized the police.

> *There were some deficiencies in the early stages of the investigation of Richard's disappearance. It is important, and accords with common sense, that in an investigation involving a suspicious disappearance, it is the hours, days and weeks following the disappearance that*

represent the best opportunity to gather crucial evidence. This is the most important time for focusing available resources, and securing evidence of the last known movements of the person, and evidence which might suggest possible theories as to what has happened to them.

While in Mr Sajko's case, a number of important steps were taken e.g., a media release, and some canvassing and statements, a number of opportunities to gather potentially crucial evidence were missed. I do not propose to set them out in detail as this is an ongoing investigation and it would be inappropriate for me to comment on the evidence or that any offence may have been committed by any person.[3]

There was little reporting of the coroner's verdict. It was a minor story, just an update on some old news.

■ ■ ■

Frank Mennilli became one of the most powerful men in the New South Wales Police Force. An Assistant Police Commissioner, he oversaw a major task force investigating gangland killings and he was at one stage a candidate for the top job of Police Commissioner. He survived a minor scandal a few years ago when he was alleged to be offering journalists inside information on police operations in return for favourable media coverage. He strongly denied the allegations, saying they were part of a campaign to discredit police in his region.

John Tuiletufuga was deported to his native New Zealand three years after Richard's disappearance. He was sent home after a string of criminal convictions in Australia. At the time of the Sajko inquest in 2014, Australian media went looking for Tuiletufuga in Auckland. They found him at Waitakere district court where he was facing three counts of threatening to kill and one of assaulting a police officer.

When he was spotted outside court — dressed in a tracksuit, sunglasses and beret — TV crews pursued him and his friends down an alleyway and into a car park. He tried to drive away from the reporters but discovered his car had been clamped. He ran into an electrical store chased by the press pack who shouted questions. 'How would you feel if your children had disappeared? Do you know what happed to Richard Sajko?' He did not answer. Journalists told him the story wouldn't go away. But it did. Curiously, in the Waitakere case, one of the police witnesses had mysteriously failed to turn up in court. Tuiletufuga is still living in New Zealand.

Rozi Sajko is still living in the family home in Sydney. She no longer has any hope that anyone will be caught and prosecuted for the murder of her son.

FREEDOM OF INFORMATION ACTS: WHY THEY OFTEN OFFER NO FREEDOM AND NO INFORMATION

My journalism students used Australian Freedom of Information Acts to attempt to find out new information on the Sajko story. In another investigation, they attempted to find out how local councils in the state of New South Wales were spending ratepayers' money. After I lectured these students about freedom of information, many of them did what students are prone to do and went straight to Wikipedia, where they read, 'Freedom of information is an extension of freedom of speech, a fundamental human right recognized in international law.'

They discovered that Freedom of Information Acts in democracies are based on a right to know, a government's information is your information and as a citizen you are entitled to it. They discovered more than 70 countries have Freedom of Information Acts, that they are long established in countries like the UK, US, Canada, Australia and New Zealand, and that they can be used by journalists to get information for their stories. The best students were inspired — the Acts seem to provide an undreamt-of source of information.

Then the students started on their Freedom of Information Act assignments and within weeks, or months, depending on their attitude and level of competence, most had given up in despair. Freedom of Information Acts should be a tool that journalists and other citizens can deploy against governments and corporations who suppress or distort the truth. But they are not working as they were designed.

I once received the result of a freedom of information request, sent to my then home in the United Kingdom. It was from the CIA, and I was delighted to get it. I hadn't expected a reply. When I opened the large package it was page after page with the title and page number and every other word blacked out, redacted.

Of course, I should not have been surprised. There are legal exemptions in every version of a Freedom of Information Act for more sensitive information, like intelligence operations or confidential financial data. As a journalist, you don't expect the CIA to be helpful. But as my students in Australia discovered, you can also be given the runaround by tiny parish councils in rural New South Wales and Victoria.

Stephen Davis,
head of journalism,
Macleay College,
Level 1, 28 Foveaux
Street SURRY HILLS
NSW 2010

Dear Mr Davis

I refer to The Newsroom's request for a review of a decision made by Moree Plains Shire Council. This letter sets out our findings following our assessment of the review request. In summary, we find that Council made a reviewable decision under section 80(a) of the Government Information (Public Access) Act 2009 (GIPA Act). The reviewable decision made by Council is that The Newsroom's access application was invalid. We have conducted the review and find that Council's decision was justified under the GIPA Act. The reasons for our findings are set out in this letter.

A copy of this letter has also been sent to the Council, so they are aware of the outcome of The Newsroom's request for review.

We have considered correspondence provided by The Newsroom and the Council in the conduct of this review.

The Newsroom's access application

On 12 September 2013, the Newsroom wrote to the Council and requested access to the following information under the Government Information (Public Access) Act 2009 (GIPA Act):

... for the financial year ending 30 June 2012:

- *A breakdown of the Mayor and each councillor's total expenses for the 2011- 2012 financial year. The Newsroom is aware that 'Councillor Expenses' are included in the council's Annual Financial Statement, but we are requesting a specific breakdown listing what and how the money has been spent.*

- *A breakdown of the Mayor and each councillor's travel and entertainment expenses for the 2011-2012 financial year. We are requesting more detail than listed under in [sic] the*

Bureaucrats in action. From the Information and Privacy Commission of New South Wales to The Newsroom, Macleay College, the student-run online site.

Translating the bureaucratic jargon: the council wanted us to pay a fee to access the information. We were trying to get details on the council's spending of ratepayers' money, an obvious matter of public interest. We did not wish to pay for information we thought the public was entitled to. Of more than 160 councils we approached, only three gave us the information we asked for. Others hid behind the fee system. They could have simply waived the fee and told us how they were spending your money but they chose not to. And in each of these cases the IPC, the Information and Privacy Commission, found for the council. So much for freedom of information. It is a small illustration of a serious problem.

Freedom of Information Acts in Australia and elsewhere are no longer functioning the way they were intended. Governments all over the world have moved to make them more restrictive. Charging for information on how your own money is spent is one way they make it harder for the public (members of the public are entitled to use the Act as well as journalists).

The idea of the charge, we are told, is to reflect the time taken to answer the requests and to discourage frivolous inquiries. Of course, governments and councils could streamline the process and reduce their level of paperwork by simply publishing all the information in the first place, without waiting to be asked. Let the public judge what is or isn't important, not civil servants. But that would put them under a level of scrutiny they are not used to and might lead to awkward questions about how public money is being spent.

Another fault of the Freedom of Information Acts is the huge bureaucracies that have been built up to administer them. This makes the whole process between first applications, responses and appeals time consuming and exhausting. Only the best-funded media organizations with the most determined journalists are prepared to spend months or even years to get results. Even then you can be stonewalled. Ask for a government memo on a controversial decision — if the words you use don't match exactly the document you are looking for, it can be rejected. No, we don't have the cabinet office memo of 12 July — it turns out it was a meeting of a sub-committee of the cabinet office.

Freedom of information will continue to be a fig leaf to cover the suppression of information the public is entitled to, until enough citizens realize that the information is theirs and that it's held by their government and other organizations that are publicly accountable, and they start to demand that their elected representatives improve the laws.

5. From the toolbox: Create your own reality

STATE-SPONSORED STORIES AND OTHER DISTRACTIONS

IN THE NEWS, 28 JANUARY 2018

Meghan to break wedding tradition

Fans embrace Oprah and Reese Witherspoon's extra appendages

Tokyo crypto exchange to replace $577m lost to hackers

New revelations about FBI secret society

It was a simple text message between lovers and not intended to be read by anyone else. It was sent just after Donald Trump had been elected President of the United States. 'Are you even going to give out your calendars? Seems kind of depressing. Maybe it should just be the first meeting of the secret society,' FBI lawyer Lisa Page wrote to senior FBI agent Peter Strzok, who was working on the FBI's probe into Russian meddling in the presidential election and possible collusion between the Russians and the Trump campaign.[1]

The message followed others between Strzok and Page that had revealed how each of them disliked Trump and did not want him to be president. Strzok had called Trump an idiot and was removed from the investigation by special counsel Robert Mueller after the messages were discovered. Now another one of the messages had been revealed and it appeared to confirm what some Republicans always suspected: that a group of FBI agents working on the Russian inquiry were out to get Donald Trump. Senator Ron Johnson of Wisconsin told Fox News about the message and declared that a source had told the Senate about secret meetings that involved the FBI.

New York Post columnist Michael Goodwin was in a state of high excitement.

> *Each day brings credible reports suggesting there is a massive scandal involving the top ranks of America's premier law enforcement agency. The reports, which feature talk among agents of a 'secret society' and suddenly missing text messages, point to the existence both of a cabal dedicated to defeating Donald Trump in 2016 and of a plan to let Hillary Clinton skate free in the classified email probe. If either one is true — and I believe both probably are — it would mean FBI leaders betrayed the nation by abusing their powers in a bid to pick the president.[2]*

He quoted another one of the Strzok–Page texts. 'I want to believe the path you threw out for consideration in Andy's office — that there's no way he gets elected — but I'm afraid we can't take that risk. It's like an insurance policy in the unlikely event you die before you're 40,' Strzok wrote. What was this mysterious insurance policy? An insurance policy in case Trump got elected? Perhaps it was the workings of the secret society, trying to overthrow the presidency of Donald Trump?

■ ■ ■

Most of the tools described in this book involve the truth being suppressed or distorted about events that actually happened. Real information is obscured by conspiracies, whistleblowers are attacked and delaying tactics employed, all in an effort to prevent awkward questions being asked and answered. But we live in a world where, thanks to the internet, people will happily share information without knowing whether it's true or not, a world where it's easy to invent your own stories and spread them to thousands or millions of people.

So here is a powerful new tool: if you are threatened by facts, invent your own. If investigations are threatening your status or grip on power, create your own reality and get your supporters to believe it. It works surprisingly well, whether for a Russian dictator or the President of the United States. Donald Trump had been accused of colluding with the Russians in the run-up to his election as they sought to boost his chances while undermining those of Hillary Clinton.

He was threatened by the law, by FBI agents and judges. So he and his supporters created their own alternative reality — with a little character assassination thrown in for good measure: there was a secret society of FBI agents who were out to get him. Fox News seized on the story. There were 90 mentions of the secret society on Fox in 24 hours, using sinister words such as 'covert' and 'cabal' to describe this supposed clandestine group. Fox News commentator Sean Hannity said that a recent treasure trove of text messages exchanged between FBI officials revealed a covert secret society at the bureau, suggesting a cabal of officials at the Department of Justice sought to oppose President Trump the day after his election.

DailyCaller.com reported, 'Senator confirms existence of FBI secret society. Says he has informant.' As the story spread, a few commentators and late-night comedians pointed out that if you were going to set up a secret society you would be unlikely to call it a secret society nor, if you were an experienced lawyer or FBI agent, would you talk about it on the phone or send text messages about it.

The reference to calendars turned out to be Vladimir Putin-themed calendars that Strzok planned to hand out as a joke. Maybe the whole text was a joke? Senator Johnson backtracked slightly — agreeing the text was probably a joke — but stuck to his claim that an informant had described off-site meetings. He and his office refused to answer any questions about the so-called informant or provide any details.

Robert Gates, the former secretary of defence and CIA director, said the notion that Justice Department officials and FBI agents were involved in a secret society to undermine the Trump White House 'does not comport with reality'. But the story rolled on and reporter Sara Carter pointed to the reference to an insurance policy. 'Their worst nightmare has come true, the president is elected. That is something they did not expect. FBI sources said from the very beginning that they didn't want Trump to make it into office.'

In a Fox interview, she added her own twist. 'I'm concerned that they're still working at the FBI,' Carter said. 'I'm hearing from my sources, too, FBI agents are saying, Why are they still there? The Lovebirds? They were having an affair, they were both married, and they're working counter-intelligence. That's enough for blackmail,' Carter said. 'Now they're sending text messages on an unsecured phone. Believe me, the Germans, the Russians, the Israelis, everybody is going into those phones and trying to suck out all the information they have.'

By the end of the week, the House Republicans' top investigator, Trey Gowdy, was calling for Strzok and Page to testify to settle concerns over whether they were powerful enough to take down the President. Gowdy declined to say whether he thought the secret society text was a joke or real, but he added: 'Republicans are better served by letting the texts speak for themselves. These witnesses need to come in and tell us what they meant by it.'

Others spread the story, even while admitting they did not know whether it was true. The accusations of the FBI's alleged bias against Donald Trump have 'certain grounds', Wall Street analyst Charles Ortel said on a site called Sputnik. Whether or not some sort of anti-Trump FBI cabal really exists, there certainly has been something rotten within the agency's senior ranks over the past decades, he said. Curiously, Ortel was described as an investigative reporter even though on his own site he called himself an investor writer. In cyberspace, the story just got bigger and bigger, with headlines such as, 'Thousands of new Strzok–Page messages reference SECRET SOCIETY' and 'Dick Morris: FBI secret society plotted Trump overthrow'.

The story reached Infowars, a website and radio broadcast with millions of followers, run by the conspiracy theorist Alex Jones. Among the conspiracies that Jones has propagated is that a gunman's mass murder of twenty schoolchildren at Sandy Hook elementary school in Newtown, Connecticut, was a hoax. His theory — without a single fact to support it — has led to a campaign of abuse and death threats against the grieving parents.

Infowars added even more dramatic twists to the secret society story, as it reported:

> The secret society that is attempting to bring down President Trump includes federal judges, former Attorney Generals and one sitting Attorney General of a large US state and its members are using burner phones to evade detection, according to a new report. On Monday, Rep. John Ratcliffe (R-TX) revealed that congressional investigators learned from a new batch of text messages between anti-Trump FBI investigators Peter Strzok and Lisa Page that a secret society within the DOJ and the FBI had schemed immediately after Trump's election win to undermine the President.
>
> That secret society doesn't just include rogue anti-Trump FBI agents but also federal judges, federal prosecutors, one sitting Attorney General of a large US state and, potentially, former Attorney General(s) of the United States, according to a new report. They communicate with meetings over cocktails, at homes, via encrypted chat rooms, texting on drug-cartel-inspired burner phones, and even via an email list, according to sources. Others have secured phones in the names of relatives to try to stay under the radar. The group recently became more paranoid about its communications being monitored after it became clear that the 'deep state' plot to sabotage Trump could unravel following Peter Strzok being exposed last month.

Archives of *The Times of London* and *The Sunday Times* contain millions of words' worth of stories, national and international, from the papers' long and distinguished histories. Search for the words 'FBI secret society' and you get 9354 results — none of them about an actual secret society at the FBI. If you Googled the same three words after the made-up story broke you got 6,460,000 results in 0.61 seconds. It is easy to dismiss the secret society story as paranoid nonsense and to laugh at its absurdity and the accompanying hype often promoted by elected representatives who should know better. Supposed reporters quoting other people quoting Twitter accounts that are quoting other dubious sources, and all over a single text message which is clearly a joke.

But the fake story served its purpose, which was to distract people from the actual investigation into well-documented allegations of collusion between the Trump campaign and the Russians and evidence that the Russians had deployed internet bots and trolls to influence the election in favour of Trump. It was part of a campaign to discredit the FBI and, at least among Trump supporters, it worked. The absence of something (that, in this case, was missing text messages) added to the illusion of something real happening. President Trump himself tweeted that the missing messages were 'one of the biggest stories in a long time'. (The messages later turned up and contained little of interest.)

The story may have been investigated and dismissed by mainstream media outlets but that only added to the conviction of Trump supporters that journalists were out to get him. The reports denouncing the secret society story were fake news, the denials were just a cover-up and the real conspiracy was ongoing — and could be found, and explained, on any number of online sites and Twitter accounts.

It was like a shape-shifting alien in a Hollywood movie, taking on many forms, impossible to kill. For secret society, read 'deep state'. For insurance policy, read 'plan B'. The 50,000 missing FBI text messages that went 'missing' but were then found were said to contain threats of violence aimed at President Trump. The messages contained 'frightening conversations' that went further than just harming Trump politically.

'Evidence' that the government was plotting to kill its own president came from counter-terrorism analyst and former CIA agent Philip Mudd who said on CNN: 'the government's gonna kill Donald Trump.' (This was widely repeated as a real threat despite the fact that Mudd was clearly using an over-the-top phrase to describe how Washington officials were reacting to Trump's policies, which they opposed. He went on to say, 'He defends Vladimir Putin. There are State Department and CIA officers coming home, and at Langley and Foggy Bottom, CIA and State, they're saying, "This is how you defend us?"')

NRA TV, the channel of the National Rifle Association, was still discussing the secret society weeks later. For people living in their Facebook and Twitter filter bubbles, excluding themselves from other points of view and facts, these kinds of wild stories don't just run alongside real news but can replace them. The fabricated story is still out there and no doubt still believed by many.

BOTS AND TROLLS ARE DEPLOYED TO SPREAD FALSE INFORMATION

A troll is a real person who posts things on the internet designed to provoke or upset people, starting arguments and whipping up emotions and distracting people from the issue they were discussing. A troll tries to turn factual conversations into something else. These trolls can be perpetuated by individuals for their own perverse motives but they are also employed by state actors, often Russia, to influence public debates.

An internet bot, short for web robot, is a software application that runs automated tasks (scripts) over the internet. The tasks are simple and repetitive and done at a much faster rate than a person could achieve. The most common use of bots is in web crawling, in which an automated script fetches, analyzes and files information at many times the speed a human could achieve. It is estimated that more than half of all web traffic is made up of bots. Bots can be good — helping internet searches — but they can also be used to spread malicious, distorted or completely untrue information with incredible speed and reach, to influence public debate in political campaigns or discussions about other controversial issues on social media channels like Facebook and Twitter.

Bots and trolls were deployed in the US presidential election campaign of 2016 but they have also been used in

Europe to whip up anti-immigrant fervour and in campaigns against European integration. They were deployed, for instance, in support of the Brexit campaign in Britain and on behalf of the extreme right-wing candidacy of Marine Le Pen for French president.

■ ■ ■

Those who deploy the 'create your own reality' tool would like to make awkward facts go away, replacing them with their own 'facts'. But if they can't do that, they can deploy a variation: create multiple alternative realities so citizens are not sure which of several possible versions of an event are actually true.

Sergei Skripal was a former Russian intelligence officer who spied for the British, as a double agent. He was exposed in 2004 and tried by the Russians for high treason, and sentenced to thirteen years in prison. Six years later he was freed as part of a spy swap, and settled into a comfortable retirement in the United Kingdom. On 4 March 2018 he and his daughter Yulia, who was visiting him from Moscow, were found slumped on a park bench near a shopping centre in Salisbury, England. Authorities quickly determined the couple had been poisoned with a nerve agent. A police officer sent to check on Skripal's house also fell ill from poisoning. The nerve agent was quickly identified as Novichok, developed in a secret Russian laboratory.

Suspicion fell on Russian authorities. They made the nerve agent, they were the only ones with a logical motive and there was a history of murders of opponents of the regime living abroad. The UK and other countries in the West retaliated by expelling Russian diplomats and spies. The Russian response was a textbook example of sowing confusion. They didn't just deny the crime and stick to one story — they produced multiple alternatives.

First up, the embassy in London and Sergei Lavrov, the Russian foreign minister, claimed a Swiss laboratory had identified the poison as a toxin called BZ, not Novichok. Russia did not have BZ. The US, UK and NATO had the poison. Second, the Russians said the British had destroyed the real evidence and were making false claims. Third, they said the Skripals were not poisoned at all and fourth, that Yulia had been abducted and hidden from public view and injected with unnamed chemicals before the poison tests were carried out so therefore the results were wrong.

Even more theories were spread online by Russian trolls and their supporters including, inevitably, one that said the Israelis did it (in online conspiracy theories, there is almost always one version blaming Israel — no matter how improbable politically and geographically).

The Guardian newspaper in the UK commented on the Russian tactics, saying, 'The Skripal case vividly illustrates how the Kremlin has abandoned conventional diplomacy. Its foreign emissaries are now full-time trolls, with the ambassador to the UK, Alexander Yakovenko, personally approving many tweets. Moscow's tactics include sarcasm, denial, innuendo and noisy counter-accusation.'[3]

The tactic had been used when paramilitaries supported by the Kremlin fired a Russian-supplied missile that destroyed Malaysia Airlines flight MH17 in mid-air as it flew over eastern Ukraine, killing all 298 people on board. Russian TV broadcast a number of theories, including that the plane had been shot down by a Ukrainian fighter pilot, that it was a CIA plot and that the passengers were already dead before the plane was shot down.

It didn't matter how bizarre some of the theories were, and the more the merrier. They cast a seed of doubt internationally and, more importantly, inside Russia itself, where state propaganda has brainwashed many of its citizens to believe in outlandish anti-Russian plots cooked up by the West. Indeed, the Russian people are the victims of truth distortion and suppression on a frightening scale.

Anne Applebaum, the distinguished author, columnist and Russia expert, summed up one analysis of the output of state-run Russian TV:

> *Most of the stories, ranging from big news events to local murders to sheer inventions ('the German government is taking children away from their families and giving them to gay couples') fit into a particular set of narratives. Daily life in Europe is depicted as frightening and chaotic; Europeans are weak, with declining morality and no common values; terrorism keeps people paralyzed with fear; the refugee crisis is getting worse all the time; sanctions on Russia have backfired and are now undermining the European economy and destroying the welfare state. Russia, in the version of the world depicted here, does not need a welfare state, since its citizens are so much hardier.*
>
> *This research echoes earlier studies, such as one that also noted how often the European Union is shown by Russian media as aggressive and interventionist, alternately planning to use Ukraine as a dumping ground for nuclear waste or forcing its members to adopt Russophobic policies. The uses of this kind of coverage aren't hard to guess. Clearly, it is not in the Russian state's interest for the*

Russian nation to admire Europe, not for its democracy or its rule of law, and certainly not for its high standards of living.

The memory of the Maidan protest of 2014 — young Ukrainians protesting in Kiev, waving European flags and calling for an end to corruption — is still fresh enough to be frightening in Moscow. If the Putin regime can undermine the idea of 'Europe' and make it unattractive to Russians, most of whom have long identified themselves as Europeans, then it removes a source of hope, and a possible model. If Europe is crazy, twisted, dangerous and dying, then surely Russians are better off under their corrupt authoritarian system.[4]

The political tactics of invention are no longer the preserve of dictatorships with state-controlled media. They are frequently deployed in the United States on controversial issues, such as immigration or, rather, fear of immigrants. In November 2017, Fox News reported what appeared to be an appalling crime.

Illegal immigrants appeared to have 'ambushed' two US Border Patrol agents near the Texas border with Mexico and bashed their heads with blunt objects, possibly rocks, killing one agent and sending another to a hospital in a serious condition Sunday, a National Border Patrol Council (NBPC) official told Fox News.

Brandon Judd, the president of the NBPC, said it appeared the agents were 'ambushed' by a group of illegal immigrants. 'We don't know exactly what happened because we weren't there. However, just from agents that were working in the area, reports are saying it was an attack and it would appear to be an ambush.'

Judd added: 'There's a high likelihood this was an assault on the agents.'

Texas governor Greg Abbott offered a US$20,000 reward for information leading to the arrest and conviction of 'the person or persons responsible' for the attack. The National Border Patrol Council is the union for border patrol agents. They were understandably concerned about the death. But note that the statement says they did not know what happened.

Donald Trump, one of the most avid viewers of Fox News, quickly followed suit with a tweet: 'Border Patrol Officer killed at Southern Border, another badly hurt. We will seek out and bring to justice those responsible. We will, and must, build the Wall!'

Most reports began to refer to the death as murder. A Fox News host said the agent had died in the most gruesome way possible, beaten to death with rocks. At a cabinet meeting with the cameras rolling, President Trump said the officer had been brutally beaten and that 'we are going to have that wall'. The death led to a major FBI investigation involving 37 field officers. Months later, it announced that its inquiry 'has not conclusively determined' what happened but that 'none of the more than 650 interviews completed, locations searched, or evidence collected and analyzed have produced evidence that would support the existence of a scuffle, altercation, or attack on 18 November 2017.' No suspects had been linked to the incident.[5]

The report went on to reveal that there had been calls from one of the agents to a dispatcher. 'We ran into a culvert', 'I ran into a culvert' or 'I think I ran into a culvert,' he said. The call showed it was almost certainly a traffic accident.

There is zero evidence that any crime was committed, never mind a murder, still less one committed by stone-wielding illegal immigrants trying to cross the border. Fox News buried the FBI report and continued to carry the story about the agents having their heads bashed in with blunt objects. President Trump did not correct his tweet. The fake news story is still out there.

■ ■ ■

Our news values are being shaped by maths, by the algorithms used by social media to determine what we see and what we don't. These algorithms on Twitter and Facebook can be hijacked and used by one country against another — fake news as information warfare. It is now well established that Russia tried to influence the 2016 US presidential election with propaganda spread by social media which promoted Donald Trump and denigrated Hillary Clinton. What is less well known is Russian attempts to stir up racial hatred.

The University of Missouri in Columbia is home to one of the world's best journalism schools. During two visits there on study trips as a guest lecturer, it struck me as the most peaceful and friendly of college towns, so I was surprised when in late 2015 there was a series of conflicts on campus over race. What was shocking, however, was how quickly the dispute escalated, hostilities spread, and it became a global news story. It turned out that wasn't by accident.

A hashtag called #PrayforMizzou began trending and quickly reached the top of news feeds with the sensational development that the Ku Klux Klan was marching on campus, alongside the police. A user called Jermaine said they had beaten up his little brother and sent out a picture of a black child with a bruised face. The story spread quickly and journalists began arriving to find the KKK marchers and cover the violence. But none of it was real.

US Air Force Lieutenant Colonel Jarred Prier, in a study on social media as information warfare, explained.

> *Looking at Jermaine's followers, and the followers of his followers, one could observe that the original tweeters all followed and retweeted each other. Those users also seemed to be retweeted automatically by approximately 70 bots. These bots also used the trend-distribution technique, which used all of the trending hashtags at that time within their tweets, not just #PrayforMizzou. Spaced evenly, and with retweets of real people who were observing the Mizzou hashtag, the numbers quickly escalated to thousands of tweets within a few minutes. The plot was smoothly executed and evaded the algorithms Twitter designed to catch bot tweeting, mainly because the Mizzou hashtag was being used outside of that attack.[6]*

The picture of the black child was not from Missouri but from an incident in Ohio a year earlier. But that wasn't revealed until much later and by then the damage had been done. The student president of the university tweeted a warning to stay off the streets and lock doors because 'KKK members were confirmed on campus'. TV News channels had camera crews racing through campus looking for violence. There were news reports quoting tweets describing cross burnings and shootings, none of them true.

Ironically, the media were blamed by many tweeters for not covering the violence on campus. So fake tweets about fake violence led to actual news coverage *and* attacks on the media for their lack of coverage — all around an event that did not take place. Racial tension increased, American society was made to look bad, faith in the mainstream media was weakened and it was a triumph for the Russian-developed bots that hijacked the news.

According to the study the same accounts were later used to spread anti-Islamic and anti-European Union propaganda in debates over immigration. Prier's study is significant. The involvement of military is a pointer to a future in which the war on truth won't just be an issue for citizens in individual countries but will be fought like a real war between nations. Military planners all over the world are already preparing for these information wars. 'For years, analysts in the defense and intelligence communities have warned lawmakers and the American public of the risks of a cyber Pearl Harbor,' Prier wrote.

The fear of a widespread cyber-based attack loomed over the country following intrusions against Yahoo! email accounts in 2012, Sony Studios in 2014, and even the United States government Office of Personnel Management (OPM) in 2015. The average American likely did not understand exactly how, or for what purposes, US adversaries were operating within the cyber domain, but the implications of future attacks were not difficult to imagine. Enemies of the United States could target vulnerable power grids, stock markets, train switches, academic institutions, banks, and communications systems in the opening salvos of this new type of warfare.

But Prier pointed to another kind of attack:

In contrast to more traditional forms of cyberattack, cyber operations today target people within a society, influencing their beliefs as well as behaviours, and diminishing trust in the government. US adversaries now seek to control and exploit the trend mechanism on social media to harm US interests, discredit public and private institutions, and sow domestic strife. 'Commanding the trend' represents a novel and increasingly dangerous means of persuasion within social media. Thus instead of attacking the military or economic infrastructure, state and non-state actors outside the United States can access regular streams of online information via social media to influence networked groups within the United States.

In the case of the 'secret society', the strategy of creating your own reality worked in that it convinced the true believers, stoking fears in the heartland of Trump voters that the FBI really is out to get him. The border patrol 'murder' was useful in pushing the anti-immigrant agenda. The Russian bots in Missouri worked because the fake news spread faster and wider than coverage in the mainstream media. Old-fashioned reporting skills and principles fell victim to the demands of social media.

Russian disinformation campaigns in Europe worked because they sowed confusion and doubt. The truth could be found in any of these stories, if you wanted to find it. But other truth-prevention tools have been much more successful in deceiving journalists of all stripes in covering up the most appalling government blunders. How, for instance, do you explain why you landed a planeload of civilians in a war zone?

6.
From the toolbox:
Manufacture another truth

THE HUMAN SHIELDS — HOW A COVER-UP WAS COVERED UP

IN THE NEWS, 1 AUGUST 1990

Duck tales: the quest for gold is best-selling video game
Cleveland Indians' Alex Cole sets club record with five stolen bases in one game
Iraq pulls out of talks with Kuwait

The Chappell family — husband John, wife Maureen and children John, fourteen, and Jennifer, twelve — settled down in their business-class seats. John was returning with his wife to India, where he was working as an electronics systems adviser to the Indian Navy. The children were on holiday from boarding school. It was early evening at Heathrow on Wednesday, 1 August 1990, and British Airways flight BA149 was bound for Kuala Lumpur, Malaysia, via Kuwait and Madras.

Departure had already been delayed for two hours and it seemed to put passengers and crew on edge. Jan Bhatt, an American engineer, was looking forward to a reunion with the family he had left behind when he emigrated from India. Bhatt was not a healthy man, as he suffered from high blood pressure and diabetes, but he had brought his medicines in his bag in the hold of the plane.

Kuwait is two hours ahead of London time and as BA149 waited on the tarmac, the Medina and Hammurabi armoured divisions of Iraq's spearhead Republican Guard were turning over the engines of their battle tanks, keeping them warm in the cold air of an Arabian night some 4800 kilometres (3000 miles) away in the desert just north of the Kuwait border. The Republican Guard troops were the pride of Saddam Hussein's regime and were recruited mostly from the areas around Tikrit, the power base and family fiefdom of Saddam. They were among the best-paid and best-fed troops in the Iraqi army.

They were to be the cutting edge of Saddam's invasion of Kuwait, the dictator's way of settling a long-running dispute between the two countries over the lucrative oil fields that straddled their common border. They were well prepared and had detailed maps of Kuwaiti positions and the movement of patrols around key buildings. They had been briefed at 4 p.m. local time — five hours before BA149 finally took off. The Kuwaiti government was about to change, the officers told their men. Iraq was setting up a new government.

Between the Iraqi massed tanks and the flat expanse of Kuwait is the Mutla Ridge, the only part of Kuwait that rises above the desert. It lies 8 kilometres (5 miles) south of the border and its height masked the tanks from the prying eyes of Kuwaiti radar. But anyone who had paid attention to that morning's world news knew that the Iraqis were out there somewhere in the desert night.

Clive Earthy, the cabin services director on the British Airways flight, heard the news just after he left his home near Winchester for the early afternoon drive to Heathrow. Earthy had been flying long haul for more than twenty years and he was used to dealing with on-board dramas. Although Earthy was known at the airline for his calm and cheerful demeanour, the radio report filled him with a sense of foreboding.

Iraqi troops were on the border with Kuwait and some reports even had them across the border already and peace talks between Iraq and Kuwait were faltering. The UK's Foreign Office issued a statement that the British embassy in Kuwait was advising British nationals to keep their heads down. There was a contingency plan to evacuate them in an emergency but it was not felt that the situation yet required the plan to be put into effect.

In Kuwait City at the British embassy that afternoon, John Raine, the information officer, briefed visiting journalists that even if the Iraqi army did cross the border, it would remain in the northern half of the country. Little fighting was expected and the city was not under threat. Several of the journalists decided this was no big story and booked flights home.

The embassy then closed for the Arab weekend, Thursday and Friday. That night Ambassador Michael Weston was joined in an all-night vigil by his deputy and also a third man, Tony Paice, who had several titles, but who was best known in Kuwait's diplomatic community as the station chief for MI6. Earlier, Paice met British Airways local staff and told them officially it was safe for BA149 to fly. The same message was given to BA senior management at Heathrow.

In Washington, analysts at the Defense Intelligence Agency pored over the latest satellite photographs from southern Iraq. The most recent fly-past showed that the Iraqi army camps, home to 100,000 troops just 24 hours earlier, were now empty. All that could be seen were hundreds of tank tracks in the sand, all heading in one direction — towards Kuwait. The DIA chiefs ordered the staff to go to Watchcon One, the highest alert level.

One of the great myths of the first Gulf War — propagated by the UK and US governments — was that the Iraqi invasion caught the West by surprise. In March 1990, in a speech at the Arab League summit, Saddam had launched a savage attack on Kuwait, accusing it of waging economic war against his country and slanting its oil drills to steal oil from Iraqi fields in the border area. In the following months, the government-run Iraqi press made it clear that the regime would accept nothing less than total surrender. No peace was possible unless Kuwait agreed that it had stolen oil worth $US2.4 billion. By mid-July, the Republican Guard, observed by American satellites, was undertaking large-scale exercises in the south.

The British and US government line that it was a surprise was the first of many distortions of the truth that have surrounded this story. The fate of BA149 and its passengers has never received the attention it deserved, thanks to the deployment of multiple truth-suppression tools that mean even now, three decades later, the official, distorted version of events is the only one most people might know about.

The intelligence communities, in particular the CIA and MI6, had plenty of warning to make preparations for an invasion. And they did prepare. On 24 July 1990, eight days before Flight BA149, a handpicked group of men received special 'warning orders' from the British government. The men were from the British armed forces and

MI6, and they were on secondment to a highly secretive unit known in the trade as The Inc, short for increment. The group was told to prepare for a high-risk mission that had been approved at the highest levels of government.

One of the team was a man called John, formerly of the Special Boat Service, the maritime special forces equivalent of the SAS, the Special Air Service. John and eight other men were dressed in civvies. The team was to get into Kuwait before the invasion started and to provide human intelligence — 'humint', in the jargon of the intelligence community. This was the best kind of intelligence, better than any satellite photo or communications intercept. It was also the most dangerous.

The team was to provide 'eyes on the ground' mostly in the capital, Kuwait City, and had to be ready to call in air strikes on Iraqi positions. Detailed discussions had taken place about the best way to get the team into Kuwait. It had to be fast and reliable, and avoid awkward border crossings and checkpoints. The simplest method was to fly direct to Kuwait and the choice was a British Airways flight, 149.

■ ■ ■

John left for Heathrow by taxi on the afternoon of 1 August 1990. He checked in under his cover name. The team all carried with them radio and surveillance gear, disguised as professional camera and geophysical surveying equipment to do survey and engineering work for an oil company. It was assumed that the plane would land, refuel, disembark some of the passengers and then continue on to its next destination, Madras, before the invasion started. None of the civilians on BA149 would be any the wiser.

No weapons were taken on board. British Embassy staff in Kuwait had concealed weapons and rations in various storage places hidden around the city so that they could be collected later. They had also arranged for a couple of locals to work as baggage handlers at the airport to help the team get their gear out of the plane quickly. Vehicles were to be collected from a local car dealer just minutes away from the international airport.

John boarded the plane last, waiting in case there was any late change of orders. Despite the team's careful preparations, their last-minute arrival had attracted the interest of some of their fellow passengers and their one-way tickets caused raised eyebrows among the crew. On board were 367 passengers, including eleven children, American, British, French, Indian, Malaysian, Italian, Spanish, German and Australian, as well as one Canadian and two New Zealanders and eighteen crew.

Two of the passengers, Daphne and Henry Halkyard, were unhappy about being on the plane. The retired couple, in their sixties, were on their way back to New Zealand to their home in the riverside town of Warkworth in the North Island, after a holiday in Greece. Both were British-born but they had lived in New Zealand for over 30 years and were dual passport holders. For convenience they travelled on their British passports because they allowed visa-free access to more countries than their New Zealand ones.

Henry had served in the army in the Middle East. He had not enjoyed the experience and had no desire to return. He was alarmed to discover that the flight was scheduled to land in Kuwait for refuelling and a change of crew. The Halkyards had also heard the news about Iraqi troop movements and they expressed their worries forcefully to the British Airways check-in staff and anyone else from the airline they could find.

Aware that some of the passengers were anxious about what they had heard on the news, Clive Earthy made an announcement over the plane's PA system. 'We have been assured that it is safe to fly to Kuwait,' he told them. That was the government advice, but if problems arose the plane would be diverted. The passengers breathed sighs of relief and some even clapped. Earthy's reassuring announcement before take-off surprised Dr Paul Dieppe, a consulting physician from Bristol who was en route to Kuala Lumpur. He had been so busy with his job that he had cancelled plans to fly on Air Malaysia two days previously and at the last minute booked himself on BA149.

The flight finally took off at 7.04 p.m. UK time, 9.04 p.m. in Kuwait, and was proceeding smoothly. Earthy moved through the cabin handing out landing cards for Kuwait but when he reached the group of young men, the late arrivals, he was surprised that they appeared to be uninterested in the cards. 'We don't have time for them,' one said. 'But you will need them when you land,' Earthy insisted. The men took the cards.

■ ■ ■

On the Kuwaiti border, the Republican Guard was on the move. Near the border between Kuwait and Iraq, American technicians at a radar observation post saw Iraqi armaments coming over the Mutla Ridge — tanks and support vehicles as far as the eye could see and filling their radar screens. In Kuwait City at 1.45 a.m. local time the last aircraft to leave the country took off, a Swissair flight to Geneva. On board were the wife and young son of BA's Kuwait manager, Laurie O'Toole. He and his family were returning to Geneva just two days after they had arrived back in Kuwait from a holiday.

As BA149 flew across the Mediterranean, other Kuwait-bound flights were being turned away. There was no official alert to the Kuwaiti armed forces that an invasion was underway. The Iraqi forces met little resistance as they smashed across the border and headed rapidly south.

Britain's Prime Minister Margaret Thatcher was in Aspen, the exclusive ski resort in Colorado in the American Rockies, meeting President George Bush (senior). At 3 a.m. Kuwait time, early evening in Colorado, her foreign policy adviser, Charles Powell, phoned to tell her that the Iraqis had invaded Kuwait. Satellite photos showed that the Republic Guard's Hammurabi Division was heading straight down the main highway to Kuwait City. BA149 flew on.

In the darkness, as the plane landed to the south of the capital, passengers could see the lights of Kuwait City. At 4.13 a.m. local time, BA149 touched down for the planned refuelling stop. Seconds later the group of young military-looking men left the plane just as quickly and quietly as they had joined it. Most of the remaining passengers chose not to disembark and dozed as the cleaners boarded the plane.

George Saloom, an American banker from San Diego travelling with his wife, Deborah, and son, Preston, was due to take up a new job with a local bank. His youngest son, Nathan, had remained behind in the United States for medical treatment. When the plane landed, the family cleared immigration, a process which seemed quicker and quieter than usual and the immigration official had just one question, 'What are you doing here?' As they left the airport and headed north towards the city they heard a loud noise that sounded like thunder or maybe an explosion. They asked their driver what it was but he shrugged his shoulders and said not to worry. The radio was on, broadcasting non-stop news in Arabic.

The driver seemed nervous but he kept saying to the Salooms in broken English, 'Don't worry, don't worry'. The route to the hotel seemed circuitous and they passed several intersections where soldiers were sitting in trucks or jeeps. There was another loud bang in the distance, this time even more like an explosion. *We are in trouble*, Deborah thought. A few minutes later as they drove up to their hotel, the Meridien, they heard two loud explosions. As they hurried through to the check-in desk inside the lobby, a burst of automatic fire sprayed the street outside the hotel's front door. They turned around to see armed troops surrounding the hotel.

As twelve-year-old Jennifer Chappell stared out at the darkened airport from her window seat in business class, three fighters suddenly appeared, flying very fast and very low. Then there was a loud bang. The whole 70-metre (231-foot) length of the British Airways 747 shook violently. People jumped up from their seats, jostled each other, tried to run, shouting, 'Get out! Get out!'

As the passengers struggled to get to the tarmac the plane shook violently, its long wings flexing as explosions went off around the airport, knocking people off their feet. Iraqi forces were moving in and about the runways and MiG jets were attacking the nearby Kuwaiti

Airforce airfield. The BA149 passengers had managed to get off the plane and to the terminal, but they quickly came under the control of the invading Iraqis, who decided to load everyone onto buses and take them from the terminal to the Airport Hotel, a ten-minute ride away.

Outside the Airport Hotel there was a battle going on. From the window of her room, Jennifer looked down on the car park. She saw Iraqi tanks drive straight through it, rolling over cars, crushing them if they got in the way. She saw people in the cars trying to get out. The Iraqis did not seem to care. She called her brother over to take a look. John hadn't heard gunfire before but when he heard what sounded to him like a loud electric drill, or more accurately a series of drills, he told his sister to get down, pushing her into a crouching position beneath the level of the window. As he watched a Kuwaiti tank in the distance, something else caught his eye. It was a Kuwaiti soldier, silhouetted against the buildings as he ran across the back of the car park.

The view from the Airport Hotel.

Suddenly two Iraqi soldiers appeared and pointed their automatic weapons at the running man. They fired, emptying their magazines. It took just a couple of seconds. The Kuwaiti soldier spun, then turned as his chest exploded and he fell to the ground, dead. There was very little left of him. A stretcher arrived from somewhere to pick up the remains. *It isn't at all like the movies*, thought John. He ducked down again beneath the window with his sister. This wasn't an adventure any more. It was all too real. Real guns were being fired and real people were dying.

Meanwhile inside the Airport Hotel, as the shock of their predicament hit home, John and Maureen Chappell were thinking back to their dramatic arrival and wondering about the near-deserted state of the terminal, so unlike any of the other times they had been through the airport. There had been only one big passenger plane on the tarmac — theirs. The arrivals and departures boards had shown long lists of cancelled flights both in and out, with one exception: BA149. And for the first time the Chappells started to wonder why the plane had landed.

In the UK, as the cover-up began, relatives of the passengers who had been on BA149 were told that everything possible was being done to bring them home. The tools of deception were deployed — beginning with an outright lie. In off-the-record briefings the UK government told journalists that BA149 had made good time before the invasion had started. It was just 'bad luck' that it had been caught on the ground. In fact, Iraqi tanks had crossed the border while BA149 was still four hours' flying time from Kuwait.

Faced with a potential public relations disaster, the government manufactured another truth. Government briefings to journalists put out the narrative that the passengers were all okay, that the Iraqis were treating them well. The story made out that the passengers were being kept in luxury hotels in Kuwait, drinking cocktails by the pool in the sunshine. The hotels were putting them up for free. The delivery of hundreds of potential hostages into the hands of a dictator was like an unexpected holiday and perhaps an exciting story to tell the grandchildren.

The government was relying on the fact that it is the first version of a story that is most often believed. Get the spin out first and hope the grim aftermath does not get too much attention. Soon enough the BA149 story got lost in the major political drama that followed the invasion. But the initial deception over the flight was followed by another example of manufacturing your own truth.

In private, the UK and US governments began getting a stream of vital intelligence from the Inc teams that had landed on BA149 and from other intelligence sources. It quickly became clear that the Republican Guard was digging in for a long stay. The Iraqis began constructing huge anti-tank berms, earth walls with large ditches behind them. They were designed to be obstacles for the tanks of an attacking force. The Iraqis were preparing to defend their territorial gains in Kuwait from any counter-attack. They were not threatening to invade Saudi Arabia.

But in London and Washington, President Bush and Prime Minister Thatcher were telling the public the opposite: that the Iraqis were directly threatening to attack and then seize the Saudi northern oil fields. It was one of the justifications for the huge military deployment that was underway, Operation Desert Shield, to be followed by Desert Storm, the liberation of Kuwait by a coalition of the willing assembled by President George Bush. The arrival of US troops in Saudi Arabia had one unintended long-term consequence. A wealthy Saudi had offered to raise his own army to help kick Saddam out of Kuwait. He was angry that the kingdom was allowing Americans in — it was an insult to his faith. Osama bin Laden began plotting his revenge on the West.

■ ■ ■

The Inc team had been landed in the middle of an invasion. John and his fellow team member — name redacted — had got their bags and met up outside, making their way to a car dealer who was their contact on the ground. The plan had been to meet their support team at the warehouse complex where they would pick up the stored rations and weapons. But when they reached their rendezvous point their back-up was not there. The warehouse, and the rest of the estate, appeared to be deserted, apart from a few wild dogs barking at the new arrivals. The men sat it out for four long days. They were becoming dehydrated and their rations were running low.

On the fourth day, they heard a noise outside. John was on a toilet break but he had to freeze as a small side door swung open. In walked a Kuwaiti teenager, followed by an even younger boy. The boys told them they had been sent 'by the embassy' to help. In addition to the much-needed food and water, they brought good news: their father would be coming the following day with a tractor and trailer and he would pick the men up and take them to their objective, the town on the Saudi border. The boys' father was a farmer. He had been given permission by the Iraqis to travel around the southern part of Kuwait collecting pipes to assist the invaders with their water supplies.

The next day they climbed into a wooden box in the middle of the double trailer. The box was then covered with pipes. It was a hot and hellish journey. Once the two men were in the box and the pipes were placed over them, the farmer drove off, slowly and steadily heading south. The tractor stopped frequently at vehicle checkpoints, each time filling them with dread. Each time, the farmer produced his transit papers and was waved through. But there was no break for the two men hiding in their box.

When they reached the village, under cover of darkness they made their way to one of the old container storage areas on the farthest eastern side of town. The two men climbed into one of the containers, which was stacked on top of two others. From their hideaway it was about 500 metres (550 yards) to the main road. They had a perfect view of the long convoys of vehicles moving up and down the road and were able to send up-to-date reports on the Republican Guard movements.

In their hideout, X fell ill and began rapidly losing strength. He had food poisoning. An exfiltration was arranged, via helicopter. The pick-up point, a *wadi*, was in the middle of an empty desert that two very fit men could easily reach. But John and X were no longer two supremely fit soldiers. John was tired, hungry, thirsty and suffering from cramps but X was much worse — he was seriously ill and at times incoherent. He could hardly stand. John carried and dragged his sick comrade through the desert night, stopping every so often to read his map and compass and get his bearings, as well as to listen out for the sounds of vehicles that would signal an Iraqi patrol.

One of the team, on an earlier exercise.

To keep himself going he would pick a point on the horizon, a rock or a bump, then head for that, measuring his paces, trying to keep to a straight line although his strides were 'all over the shop'. They reached the *wadi* and John put X down and double-checked the map. They were in the right place and had arrived with twelve minutes to spare. Soon he heard the nearing sound of a helicopter flying fast and low. The CH53 took off and headed out under cover of darkness across southern Kuwait to a destroyer, the USS *Antietam*, waiting in the Gulf. As he slipped into a deep sleep — 'more like a coma' — John wondered what had happened to the rest of the mission and the passengers of BA149.

THE INCREMENT

The existence of this group, used by MI6 for deniable operations that require a special forces capability, was an open secret for many years. It still exists and is still known by many old hands as the Inc, but the modern version is called E Squadron, which was formed in 2007. Like most of these types of special force or intelligence cells, its mission is insertion into trouble spots with maximum discretion. A successful mission is one in which they get in and out without a trace. They aren't there to shoot things up or set off explosions.

At one stage, six members of the squadron were caught in Libya, a huge embarrassment for British intelligence. They were held by rebels in Benghazi before being released after high-level negotiations. There have been a number of more successful missions since, using men and women from the SAS, SBS and the Special Reconnaissance regiment, as well as intelligence officers.

■ ■ ■

The passengers and crew of BA149 had been delivered into the hands of the Iraqis. It was clear early on that, despite the spin emerging from London, they would be badly treated. The western hostages ended up at more than 70 sites all over Iraq and Kuwait, some of them nuclear and chemical research facilities, after Saddam decided to use them as human shields to deter Allied air raids. Living conditions were often appalling, and food scarce. One group was held in a container under the sluice gates of a dam.

Daphne and Henry Halkyard's decision to travel on their British rather than New Zealand passports led to them being held as human shields. Daphne recalled later:

> *Chronic fear became a way of life for us. Every day there was something on which we would focus. We were afraid of being bombed by the Allies. We were afraid of illness. We were afraid of being lynched. We were afraid of the breakdown of some of our fellow hostages. We were afraid of letting something slip that could have jeopardized members of our little group. We were watching our backs the whole time. But there was nothing we could do. Our life was on the line. We had no illusions whatsoever about that.* [1]

Jan Bhatt, the American engineer from BA149, found himself at Al Qu'am, a phosphate plant near the Syrian border. Bhatt suffered from diabetes and high cholesterol but his medicines, including allergy medicine, antigen injections and the cholesterol-reducing drug Mevacor, had all been in his checked-in baggage in the hold of the plane. He never got it back and he became progressively ill. Two 3-metre (10-foot) high barbed wire fences with armed guards protected the plant.

The prisoners quickly dubbed the area in between the fences 'the killing fields', after they were told that they would be shot if they tried to escape or if they were ever found in that area. Bhatt began to suffer from diarrhoea due to the lack of nutrition and clean drinking water. They were forced to drink dirty water to survive. They were confined to their living quarters for all but two hours a day.

The human shields were held in captivity in appalling conditions for up to four months, depending on their nationality. When they were released, the story quickly got lost in the preparations for Desert Storm and the subsequent war. The early spin, about cocktails and swimming pools, had largely worked, backed up by outright lies.

Prime Minister Thatcher had been forced to make a statement to the Commons. 'The British Airways flight landed, its passengers disembarked and the crew handed over to a successor crew and went to their hotels. All that took place before the invasion: the invasion was later,' she said. This was blatantly untrue (and it is contradicted by the timeline given in her memoirs years later).[2]

Some time after that, when then Labour transport spokesman John Prescott took up the passengers' case, his inquiries prompted a written response from John Major, who had replaced Mrs Thatcher as prime minister. 'The British government did not attempt to influence BA's decision to operate flight BA149 on 1–2 August 1990,' Major said.[3] This statement is also misleading; BA flew after getting advice from the government that it was safe to do so.

This denial of government responsibility has been central to a cover-up that has lasted to this day; a cover-up that has employed multiple tools of truth suppression, from carefully worded official statements that amount to non-denial denials to a refusal to release documents that outline what happened; from the obscuring of dates and timelines to attempts to smear journalists investigating the story. During the course of a long investigation into the fate of British Airways flight 149 I was targeted with very skilfully produced disinformation.

The use of disinformation to muddy the waters, to divert suspicion in another direction, or to discredit investigators is a classic tool. I do not know whether I was the victim of a government-sponsored effort or simply of a private initiative by someone acting out of malice. At the centre of any investigation involving government secrets is a crucial relationship — that between a reporter and their source.

A reporter needs sources inside the secret world and needs to be able to trust them. The source needs to trust that the reporter will do their job and protect the source's identity — spies and special forces soldiers talking about secret missions are committing a crime for which they can be sent to prison. The sources that I have used for the stories in this book have been developed over a large number of years. I trust most of them.

Then there is Nigel Appleby, alias Niall Arden, alias Niall Adams. I still do not know his real name — so for the purposes of this story I will call him Nigel. There is one fact about the man called Nigel Appleby that I can be sure of. He is or was a military artist and his work involves paintings of missions of the SAS, the Special Air Service. You can buy prints online. His work was well known in the special forces community and he clearly had contacts in that area.

I had no reason to doubt his bona fides when I met him through an introduction from the publisher Andrew Lownie. He was also a contact of the well-respected author Damien Lewis. I was interested in Nigel as an intermediary to find members of the team who were on board BA149, not in Nigel himself. I already had two sources for details of the mission — I was looking for other sources. Nigel subsequently introduced me to a number of people, either in person or via email, who said they had information about the mission. I was looking to get information from them to check against what I knew.

The holy grail would be some sort of official documentation about the mission. One contact led to another then another, over a period of several years. Then one day I received an email with attached documents from a man calling himself Malcolm Anthony Pettit, whom I had been communicating with about the Inc team. All our contact had been via email and I had no idea as to his real name but the documents he sent were stunning. There were four of them and they looked like after-action reports of the BA149 mission.

AFTER ACTION/OPERATION REPORT - BRIEF

NOTE: ALL DETAILS MUST BE CLEARLY WRITTEN, DATES CORRECT AND SIGNED.

DEBRIEFED YES OR NO:	YES
OPERATION TITLE-DESIGNATION:	'OPERATION TROJAN HORSE'
DATE:	12ᵀᴴ OF FEBRUARY 1991

NAME:	PAUL BULLFORD	RANK:	TROOPER/SIGNALLER
UNIT:	G SQUADRON (SIGS TRP)	CALL SIGN:	TANGO HOTEL BRAVO 6

NUMBER OF PAGES:	1
LOCATION/THEATRE OF OPERATION:	KUWAIT - KTO-

SUMMARY:
Arrived Kuwait City International airport 2ⁿᵈ August 03:00 hrs. Invasion of Kuwait by Iraq already started as we landed. Daryl and I managed, after some interference from BA aircrew and despite them drawing attention to us, to secure our equipment and bags. We left airport with two FO operators masquerading as baggage handlers. I checked that at least four mini transponders were attached and working upon passengers as best I could but needed to exit premises fast. Were driven to vehicle pick up point where we secured our weapons as arranged. Moved to first OP and immediately started transmitting. (see attached RT's) Lost our OS towards end of second week as they had been betrayed and captured. One was shot during arrest. One female and two men all now missing. We had to move for fear they would give our position and set up new OP. To conserve batteries only transmitted once a day. Spent total of 27 days here before being compromised by locals by accident when Daryl cleared out personal waste that was becoming serious health risk for us as bags were shit, pardon the pun. FO sourced a better OP position in high rise tower block in City Centre with trusted Kuwait couple. We were stopped at VCP. Iraqi's quickly sussed we were European as we approached. I drew weapon and fired whilst running towards them enabling Daryl to secure our radios and LTD. This scared VCP Iraq's fortunately long enough for us to exfil area into back streets and hide up in mosque being renovated. Daryl convinced we could have bluffed it through position as Iraq's not certain of us but I took decision to engage and take initiative as we would have been surrounded otherwise and could not take risk of compromise as we had weapons and storyline of being engineers after this amount of time would not add up. Spent nearly five LONG months at old couples apartment sending intel on an as and when basis to confuse and throw off any radio DF operators but also to serious battery supply. Old couple managed to save day by acquiring new ones for battery attachment unit. Would have been non operational but for them. Nearly discovered by Iraqi search team on one occasion but old couple remained calm whilst we simply hid under their main bed. Second time search team arrived, we had to hide inside buildings main water tank on roof. Able to wonder streets as labourers on a few choice occasions in the final lead up to air campaign. Targeted positions for 48 hours at start of air campaign but batteries died for LTD and almost on radio. Secured more batteries and were able to act as FAC on first night of ground offensive. When US entered Kuwait City I was shot at by them. I returned warning fire above their heads until the dived for cover and yelled in English until they heard me. I shot 68 rounds total. No injuries sustained personally. Shot three Iraqi combatants at VCP. Daryl I believe shot two dead and I believe wounded a further three. Week after Kuwait City liberated we were flown by Army Lynx to Saudi FOB then on to RAF Akrotiri in Cyprus. RTU on the 11ᵗʰ of February 1991. Not seen RAF or US sat reports on FAC results.

SIGNED: *[signature]*

AUTHORISED/APPROVED: *Alan Shadworth*	RANK:	CAPT

SIGNED: *[signature]*

COMMENTS/ANY FURTHER ACTIONS:
Good sual brief. Helps as full debrief extensive & APPROVED
15-02-91

CLASSIFICATION – SECRET
WARNING. THIS IS AN OFFICIAL RESTRICTED - SECRET DOCUMENT NOT FOR PUBLIC RELEASE. IF FOUND RETURN IMMEDIATELY TO NEAREST MOD ESTABLISHMENT OR POLICE STATION. FAILURE TO COMPLY WILL RESULT IN FULL LEGAL PROCEEDINGS.

CLASSIFICATION - SECRET

AFTER ACTION/OPERATION REPORT - BRIEF
NOTE; ALL DETAILS MUST BE CLEARLY WRITTEN, DATES CORRECT AND SIGNED.

DEBRIEFED YES OR NO: *YES*

OPERATION TITLE-DESIGNATION: *TROJAN HORSE*

DATE: *23 rd August 1990*

NAME: *MATHEW MILLER*   RANK: *CPL*

UNIT: *'G' SQN 22*   CALL SIGN: *TANGO HOTEL 2*

NUMBER OF PAGES:

LOCATION/THEATRE OF OPERATION: *KUWAIT (KTO)*

SUMMARY:

Departed Heathrow on BA149 flight 18:15 for Kuwait City August 1990. After arriving at 03:00 as 2nd Regt we received an 'Surveyors' gun met our vehicle man who signed 2x M16A2's (M4) and RABBITS. In the personally. Tried to handover OP but ditched driver on way. Spent 24 hours in car watching site before setting up OP. OS a no show so waited for new instructions. Four day later were moved to Saudi/Kuwait border tent of Hafar al Batin. Set up in old Container park. I got food poisoning, by second day don't remember much more until I came to at USS Antietam. John Wilms (SGT) I believe carried me to coordinates FRV. Believe it was 4 days later we crossed to RFA supply → Then Cyprus. No casualties or Contacts. No Rounds fired. All weapons/occupied for.

SIGNED: *[signature]*

AUTHORISED/APPROVED: *Alan Shadwode*   RANK: *CAPT*

SIGNED: *[signature]*

COMMENTS/ANY FURTHER ACTIONS:

Full notes required asap. Write a transcripts attached. Should have been in ink NOT pencil.

CLASSIFICATION – SECRET

CLASSIFICATION - SECRET

AFTER ACTION/OPERATION REPORT - BRIEF
NOTE: ALL DETAILS MUST BE CLEARLY WRITTEN, DATES CORRECT AND SIGNED.

DEBRIEFED YES OR NO: **YES**

OPERATION TITLE-DESIGNATION: ~~JAN HORSE~~ *APPROVED 15-02-91*

DATE: 13-02-91

NAME: DARYL HALLET   RANK: SGT

UNIT: D SQN 22– AUGMENTEE/14INT   CALL SIGN: TANGO HOTEL SUNRAY SIX

NUMBER OF PAGES: 1

LOCATION/THEATRE OF OPERATION: KTO

SUMMARY:

Flew on flight BA 149 for Kuala Lumpur at 16:15, 1 August 1990. Arrived Kuwait 2 August 03:00 hrs. Iraq invaded Kuwait while we were still in flight. Shortly after landing we disembarked, managed to secure our kit from FO BH. Taken directly to our first OP we set up and managed to transmit, see attached RT's, intel daily. Our OS kept us supplied until second week they stopped showing at RV location four houses away from us. Later discovered they had been compromised. Their movements had aroused suspicion. Believe they were taken away, one confirmed shot at scene dead. Female and two other males taken and never seen so far. As consequence we moved to another location and set new OP. Serious problem with battery supplies so intel reduced to once a day. After 27 days second OP compromised by locals inadvertently. I was disposing of large amount of personal waste we'd accumulated as plastic bags were deteriorating so suggest stronger for next time. On move we were stopped at VCP. Had to abandon vehicle and return fire. It was just approaching curfew time so had to hide up in old Mosque under reconstruction. Iraqi's did not gauge we fired 5.56mm as never prosecuted further search as far as we ascertained. FO contacts set us up in old couples top floor flat short distance from Kuwait City centre. With steady stream of food, though minimal and batteries, we were able to stay set in OP for near on five months. One occasion had to hide in water tank on roof when Iraqi's ransacked building for second time. See attached for exact dates in full debrief notes. Old couple at great risk kept us well. Able to send intel but fear of DF operators we limited transmissions to once every four to six days. Managed on quite a few occasions to travel within city as labourers to locate Iraqi positions and strengths. Using LTD directed FAC on first two nights of air campaign and then on the first night of ground offensive before we lost battery power on LTD. Remained in situ until US forces entered Kuwait City. Paul nearly shot by US patrol in error but fortunately they were bad shots and missed before hearing his English. Helped in City for another seven days before pick up and flight to Cyprus and back to H on the 11 February 1991. Expended 46 rounds total. All equipment and weapons signed back in. No injuries sustained. Can confirm two EF's killed and one wounded, possibly three wounded during our contact at VCP. LTD confirmations see attached sat and RAF intel. Would recommend Paul for MID or other of higher merit as his actions at VCP, deliberately acting as bait drawing fire whilst I secured radio and LTD gear enabled continuation of operation.

SIGNED:

AUTHORISED/APPROVED: RANK: CAPT

SIGNED:

COMMENTS/ANY FURTHER ACTIONS:

Good brief. Move her it. Under debrief well presented. Keep with attachments. Recommend NOPA 10 years min.

AFTER ACTION/OPERATION REPORT - BRIEF

NOTE: ALL DETAILS MUST BE CLEARLY WRITTEN, DATES CORRECT AND SIGNED.

DEBRIEFED YES OR NO: *Yes*

OPERATION TITLE-DESIGNATION: *"OPERATION TROJAN HORSE"*

DATE: *23 AUGUST 1990*

NAME: *JOHN CARC WILKES*   RANK: *SGT*

UNIT: *G SQUADRON 22 REGT*   CALL SIGN: *TANGO HOTEL 2*

NUMBER OF PAGES: *ONE*

LOCATION/THEATRE OF OPERATION: *KUWAIT - KTO -*

SUMMARY:

Flew out Heathrow Airport on flight BA 149 for Kuala Lumpur at 18:15 PM on the 1st August 1990. Scheduled flight to Kuala Lumpur by way of Kuwait and Madras. Arrived on 2nd of August about 03:00 hours. We knew operation was seriously compromised as Iraq had already invaded ahead of time. After initial chaos and confusion we sourced our kit via the FG-supplied baggage handlers outside the departure lounge. Corporal Tiller and myself proceeded to vehicle RUP and after frantic negotiation acquired said vehicle complete with stores and two weapons as arranged. Travel took us most of the way to our first RV at warehouse but got spooked and soon legged it. We managed to avoid unfriendly forces until we secured our first OP. Watched it for 24 hours then occupied it. Sent sitreps, (See attached radio transcripts). Our OS never showed and alternate plans were implemented to have us moved to our FOP on Saudi/Kuwaiti border. This went well and old man with tractor took us to village on Saudi border. We sat tight for four days before legging it to Saudi border where we set up FOP in old lorry Container Park east of Hafar al Batin. We only had a few bottles of fresh water stashed in the car and two days worth of food. Got some fresh supplies from the tractor drivers family who helped us. Tiller got food poisoning from this however. Tiller kept cramping up. Order to move 12 miles to extraction point meant walking it. I carried him most of the way before we met helicopter at RV, a US Navy (Seaspray unit) CH53 chopper and flown out to US Navy Destroyer, USS Antietam CG-54. We spent a week on board before we were cross decked to a Royal Fleet Auxiliary supply ship and eventually back to Cyprus and home. Full debrief on video and full report to follow.

SIGNED:

AUTHORISED/APPROVED: *Alan Shedrocke*   RANK:

SIGNED:

COMMENTS/ANY FURTHER ACTIONS:

Full notes required asap. John's video account at times is unaudible so redone. Initial AA/OR is accept for now. Advise RTSC session.

I showed the documents to another contact, a retired SAS man of unimpeachable reputation, and he said they looked real. Later, though, I was sitting at my dining table at home re-reading a history of Operation Desert Storm and going through the timeline. The air war had started on 17 January 1991 but the ground war did not begin until a month later, and Kuwait City was not liberated by Allied troops until 27 February 1991. With a sickening feeling I re-read the dates in the documents that said 'Bullford' and 'Hallet' had been extracted after US troops entered Kuwait City on 11 February. The official approved stamp date on the documents was 15-02-91. Both dates were clearly wrong. American troops were not in the city on those dates; they arrived later.

I had the documents examined by a number of experts who agreed that someone with a little inside knowledge wrote them but had made key errors. The call sign Tango Hotel Sunray Six, for instance, should have been Tango Hotel *Sierra* Six. They would have been using military batteries so it was unlikely that the elderly couple in the apartment in Kuwait City could have obtained new ones.

It was clearly disinformation but what was the motive? To discredit me and the investigation? Plain malice? Or some other reason I was unaware of? It wasn't plain and simple fraud — no one helping me had or ever has asked for money. Later, one of my contacts told me, 'We had some people above us who actively wanted you to complete your book and documentary so that it could then be deliberately trashed and your credibility ruined and the whole story swept under the carpet once and for all. You must have realized you have opened a hornets' nest on this story and no one up the chain wanted it out in its complete entirety.'

As for Nigel Appleby, under the names Niall Arden and Adams, he had claimed himself to be a special forces solider and had written a book called *Desert Fire* about a mission to Iraq. Niall/Nigel was subsequently discredited and his book was alleged to be either a complete hoax or a mixture of fact and fiction. His own claims of a military career were challenged by members of the special forces community and he was unable to prove he was who he claimed to be. There was a claim — unverified — that he had been put up as a front-man to write the book by other secret service soldiers. The consensus was he was simply a hoaxer. He disappeared from view.

But nagging questions remained. One of the sensational after-action reports named a man called Paul Bullford. Later, another contact sent me a message that 'Bullford' was one Tremaine Kent: 'Paul Bullford = T. Kent = 22 SAS/264 SAS Signal Squadron. Army No: 24722528 Sgt T C Kent'. With the help of the BBC, I confirmed that T. Kent was still on the books of 21 SAS regiment. Kent, who was well known in the military community, now ran his own private security company in East Anglia. He confirmed to me that he was on the mission to Kuwait.

So the Bullford character was a real person, in real life named Kent. But the after-action report that was leaked to me had the wrong dates and may well have been an invention. If the intention was to leave me confused, it had certainly worked. But my investigation carried on.

THE PERILS OF
IDENTIFYING
SPECIAL FORCES
SOLDIERS

Despite the proliferation of books and movies, soldiers who work in the elite special forces units of the US, the UK, Canada, Australia and New Zealand are a discreet bunch. They seldom discuss their missions with their fellow soldiers. Their wives and girlfriends are generally kept in the dark. Very few of them will ever speak to journalists and then only after a relationship of trust is established. You get to know one and he might, just might, after a long period of time, introduce you to someone else.

The secrecy is there for operational reasons, of course, but also out of genuine concern for their personal safety. Men who have gone up against the IRA, or the Taliban, are high-value propaganda targets for terrorists. The secrecy is an opportunity for wannabees and fraudsters. Pubs in Hereford in the UK, home of the Special Air Service, attract pretty girls from the Welsh valleys who are, as one young woman who married an SAS man put it to me, looking for 'a man with a tan'. It is an easy chat-up line for someone to pretend they are SAS.

Telling the real soldiers from the fakers is made harder by the fact that SF operatives, of course, don't go around disclosing their real names to outsiders. I once had correspondence from a contact who said his name was Grahame Bennet. I was thinking of using him as a source so I asked for his real name, service details and photo. They promptly arrived:

Leonard A. Chaganis
Army service No: 522299
7 Light Infantry
23 Special Air Service Regiment (V)
32 Armoured Engineer Regiment
26 Armoured Engineer Squadron
105 Royal Engineers Regiment
72 Royal Engineers Regiment
Kings Troop
Major
1977
2000

As a double check, I looked up Leonard Chaganis and tracked him down. No, he said, it wasn't me and I have no idea why someone is using my name and no, that's not my picture. To complicate matters the photo I was sent of Bennet/Chaganis was the spitting image of a Facebook friend of the person who was now telling me he knew nothing about all this. Was this another attempt at disinformation or just someone messing around? It was impossible to say. The only sure-fire way to avoid such diverting mysteries is to rely on trusted contacts who have proved their bona fides over a number of years. And it's extremely useful if your sources have been threatened with prosecution. Then you know they are the real deal.

■ ■ ■

The search for the truth for many of the passengers of BA149 in the UK, France and the US began with lawyers. I always tell my students who want to go into investigative reporting to make lawyers their friends. When journalists are up against a huge publicly funded apparatus of truth suppression — the government — they need more than good sources and a media employer in what will be a series of uphill battles. Lawyers have the ability to take depositions under oath in lawsuits on behalf of their clients (if you lie in a deposition, you are committing perjury and can be prosecuted).

The Chappells and others pursued British Airways for compensation, in both the English and Scottish courts. British Airways told lawyers that no copy of the passenger list existed: the one on the plane was 'lost' and the one in their UK computer system 'accidentally deleted'. This was despite the legal requirement to keep a passenger list.

In the US, a legal team led by Texan Bill Neumann, an expert in compensation cases with a winning track record, joined the battle to unearth the truth. Several American compensation cases were in progress and George Saloom was one of the plaintiffs. The US lawyers discovered that British military personnel in Kuwait had been briefed about a possible invasion days before 2 August and provided with escape kits. Bill Neumann took meticulous depositions — several hundred pages of them — from British Airways' employees involved in the BA149 affair. These depositions reflected badly on British Airways.

The picture that emerged showed what seemed to be a confused response to monitoring a very dangerous and volatile situation, but it was clear that British Airways had relied heavily on information given to them that day in two crucial meetings with British embassy staff. At 6 p.m. Kuwait local time on 1 August 1990, at the British embassy, Laurie O'Toole, BA area manager for Iraq and Kuwait, met Tony Paice, First Secretary at the embassy and as such responsible for aviation security, for an update on the Iraq situation. Paice told O'Toole that the invasion would not happen.

Rather than permit potentially embarrassing depositions to be heard before a Texas jury and made public in Europe, British Airways settled in secret and paid substantial sums in excess of six figures to Neumann's clients. A French court ordered British Airways to pay at least £3 million in damages to the 61 French passengers, stating that the airline was 'entirely responsible' for the landing in Kuwait. BA appealed twice but lost both times.

The British passengers were far less fortunate. The House of Lords dismissed two appeals by BA149 passengers against BA, upholding previous British court judgments that the airline did not have a case to answer in the courts under the terms of the Warsaw Convention, which covers airline passengers. This was a victory for BA on technical grounds and it meant that evidence against BA (and the British government) could not be presented in British courts.

The scales of justice were thus unevenly balanced as far as compensation was concerned. Richard Brunyate, the captain of BA149, tried to write a book about his ordeal, based on his diaries. He found a publisher, HarperCollins, but his employer, British Airways, blocked the publication.

■ ■ ■

While making a program on the SAS for New Zealand Television, I was introduced to an SAS contact in Hereford, the regiment's home base. He told me that there was a secret team on the plane and that they worked for an ultra-secret group called the Inc, run by MI6. He said it was too dangerous for him to talk about the group but instead he introduced me to a member of the Inc, whom I met at the Green Dragon pub in Hereford. He told me he had first-hand knowledge of the organization of the BA149 mission and provided various details. One of his friends had actually been on the mission, selected for the job because of his ability to pass as an Arab. But the contact said he could not go public, as he would go to jail.

With reporter Rod Vaughan, I investigated the BA149 affair for Television New Zealand. The Ministry of Defence refused to discuss the allegations with us. British Airways agreed to an interview but then pulled out. We also talked to Bill Neumann in Houston, Texas, about his efforts to obtain a list of passengers from British Airways. He too wanted to know the identities of the mystery men on the flight. He was told they did not have a passenger list.

I later interviewed Captain Lawrence 'Larry' Eddingfield, captain of the US Navy warship, USS *Antietam*, who confirmed he had been involved in the rescue of the two Inc operatives (John and X) from southern Kuwait in August of 1990. Eddingfield has subsequently held a senior role at the Pentagon and, when I met him, had retired and was the vicar of a church in San Diego, California. He is an unimpeachable source and he gave a detailed account of a rescue mission that the

British government still claims never happened. I also spoke to Ed Ciriello, a former CIA agent who told me he had been in Saudi Arabia in August 1990 and had been told about the BA149 intelligence mission by MI6 staff in Saudi Arabia.

In a very real sense, the cover-up is still going on. The government may never admit the truth about what happened — usually falling back on the discredited convention that they do not discuss matters concerning special forces or the intelligence services (although they often do when it suits them). When asked in parliament about my investigation by Norman Baker MP, a then Labour government minister, Geoff Hoon, issued a bizarre statement. It seemed to me to fit the old Watergate template of a 'non-denial denial'. Rather than simply state that there had been no intelligence mission on BA149, Hoon said that he 'had been told' the government had not 'exploited' the flight in the way that had been alleged.

> *What I can say to the hon. gentleman is that I have looked at the evidence to date and I have personally asked both the relevant departments with responsibilities in this area whether the outline allegations are in any way justified. I am going to read out some words very carefully, which go beyond what has been said before, and should not be capable of misinterpretation. I want to make it clear that I have been told that the government at the time did not attempt in any way to exploit the flight by any means whatever.*

Later in a private conversation with Baker after the debate, Hoon chose to attack me personally. It was a classic attempt at character assassination. He told Baker that I was a fantasist, without going to the trouble of providing any actual proof. I found the description ironic

— given the source. Hoon was part of the government that used as an excuse to go to war with Iraq the completely fantastical weapons of mass destruction dossier, which include the false claim that Saddam could launch weapons of mass destruction (WMD) within 45 minutes.

The whole point about deniable operations is their deniability, and the Inc is set up to be completely deniable. Successive governments have not even been willing to admit the truth about what happened to the BA149 passengers and the other human shields *after* they fell into Iraqi hands. Many of the human shields have not recovered from their ordeal. They have suffered long-term health problems or undergone psychiatric treatment. There have been suicides and attempted suicides. Two studies published in the *British Medical Journal* highlighted the trauma of the victims, a trauma that the public is almost totally unaware of. More than half lost their jobs and careers or homes, or suffered other severe financial damage or long-term depression and illness.

The British government has kept secret for 25 years a dossier of the full horrors suffered by the human shields. This is because of confidentiality pledges allegedly given by the 1868 people interviewed for the dossier, although without exception all the hostages I talked to for this book want the truth to come out. The Operation Sandcastle report by the Military Police's special investigation branch traced people who were either in hiding or used as human shields. A police team interviewed 725 people and sent questionnaires to another 1056 people. The report contains eyewitness accounts of one murder, eight attributable deaths, up to 70 cases of mock executions and serious physical assaults, seventeen rapes and 23 sexual assaults as well as details of 80 murders of Iraqi citizens witnessed by British hostages. Three of the people held by the Iraqis who provided information have since committed suicide.

Ann Clwyd, Labour MP for the Cynon Valley and chair of the all-party human rights group, reported Geoff Hoon to the parliamentary ombudsman, for breaching the 'open government' code by not publishing the report. But nothing happened and the report remained a secret.

■ ■ ■

The shattered tail of the British Airways 747 sitting in inglorious isolation on the runway of Kuwait airport in February 1991 was one of the iconic images of the war. The image was released amid the celebrations over the liberation of Kuwait. In the wider shot, you could see the crumpled fuselage of flight 149, which flew from Heathrow to Kuwait and never returned. The picture was released with a story quoting military sources. The 747, it was said, was destroyed by the Iraqis as they fled in haste before the might of Stormin' Norman Schwarzkopf and his allied armour and air power.

The end of flight 149.

No one seems to have asked why the Iraqis, who looted everything of value that they could get their hands on, would destroy such a valuable propaganda prize rather than simply fly it to Iraq. The answer is that they did not destroy the plane. Highly placed military sources I spoke to during the investigation told me that the BA 747 was strafed by American fighter planes, perhaps in a deliberate attempt to get rid of any sensitive documents left on the aircraft.

A British passenger plane had been destroyed by Americans, but attempts to get the story into the public arena failed. *The Guardian* newspaper took a look at it and then decided the whole BA149 saga was old news. The destruction hid any remaining secrets and British Airways received a huge insurance settlement. It was not lost on the passengers and crew that BA received compensation for its destroyed plane while they were denied compensation by the courts.

Iraq 2003. While covering the invasion and its aftermath with a team from TV3, I was able to gather new information on BA149 and the human shields.

With a patrol of US marines in Baghdad. We were unilateral journalists not embedded with a unit.

THE CIA FILE

This is a summary from my investigation of the CIA's role based on testimony and quotes from senior officials and one unique public statement, which clearly shows that they issued a formal warning of war on 25 July and upgraded it to a warning of attack on 1 August as they predicted the invasion. All such information was shared with the British government, which ignored these warnings when it allowed British Airways to fly to Kuwait on 1 August and thus put the passengers at risk.

On 25 July, CIA Director, William Webster, briefed President Bush and top officials that the intelligence community was issuing a formal 'warning of war'. The warning was based on troop movements, not on special knowledge of Hussein's intentions. The degree of military mobilization indicated that Iraq would be capable of advancing through Kuwait and deep into Saudi territory, CIA reported. The intelligence community did not predict where Hussein would strike, where he would stop, or what he intended to do; but it did warn that an attack was coming.

On 1 August the intelligence community upgraded its formal 'warning of war' to a 'warning of attack' — meaning fighting was imminent. A committee of senior officials called The Deputies Committee hastily convened a meeting. Richard Kerr, the deputy head of the CIA, was asked to estimate the chance of an Iraqi attack on Kuwait. Kerr said the probability was '99.9' per cent. In the early morning of 2 August before the sun rose, thousands of Iraqi troops and hundreds of their tanks began a rapid conquest of Kuwait. William Webster, in retirement, outlined the timeline in a little noticed speech on intelligence operations at Texas A&M University. And Richard Kerr confirmed what happened in an unprecedented public statement defending the agency:

LETTER TO NY TIMES FROM RICHARD KERR (CIA)

To the Editor:

The Once and Future C.I.A.' (editorial, Oct. 18) asserts the Central Intelligence Agency 'has, at least to public perception, flunked'. To support this assertion, you suggest the agency failed to anticipate the fall of the Berlin Wall, Saddam Hussein's aggression and the implosion of the Soviet Union. This portrayal of the agency's performance is inaccurate, and does a disservice by furthering a perception that is flat-out wrong.

. . . .

Concerning Saddam Hussein, the C.I.A. clearly warned of his potential for aggression. Longer-range estimates judged that the apparent restraint in Iraqi foreign policy following the war with Iran reflected the realities facing post-war Iraq rather than a fundamental shift in Saddam Hussein's policies or regional ambitions. During the spring of 1990 we tracked Saddam Hussein's increasingly threatening tone and behavior; in the days leading up to the invasion of Kuwait we reported the buildup of Iraqi forces on the border, and *we gave explicit warning of the possibility of attack more than a week before it occurred.*

. . . .

Any attempt to assess the C.I.A.'s performance based on the simplistic criteria of 'success or failure' trivializes the contribution of intelligence to the understanding of issues. No one can predict the future precisely, and no organization is perfect, but C.I.A.'s track record stands up to scrutiny — and our Congressional oversight committees provide it. I welcome that scrutiny and stand by our record. I commend it to those who, out of ignorance or malice, are so quick to disparage and dismiss the work this agency has done and is doing on the most complex and challenging issues of our time.

RICHARD J. KERR
Acting Dir. of Central Intelligence Langley, Va., Oct. 18, 1991

The cover-up of what happened to BA149 has largely succeeded. Any new information is dismissed as a variation of an old story, as the news editor of *The Guardian* once told me. Old news. The passengers' suffering has never got the publicity it deserved, even though the ordeal left many of them scarred for life. It is outrageous that the truth has been suppressed for so long and that so many lies have been told to the victims. Most of all, it is unforgivable that most of their suffering has been ignored.

Investigative reporting often means finding out only part of the truth, as in the BA149 story. The whole truth can remain elusive, especially when investigating something that happened in a remote location, like the icy wastes of the Antarctic.

7. From the toolbox:
The value of distance

AN ANTARCTIC RESCUE AND THE DEATH OF A SCIENTIST

IN THE NEWS, 29 DECEMBER 2016

**World shocked by Debbie Reynolds' death
a day after daughter Carrie Fisher
Obama administration announces plans to
punish Russia for election meddling
Putin announces Syria ceasefire
Massive 'anomaly' found beneath the
surface of Antarctica. Scientists
believe it could be an asteroid.**

It was nearly dark and visibility was close to zero on the runway carved from the ice at McMurdo Station, Antarctica. There were only a few lights to guide the Royal New Zealand Air Force Hercules as it descended. The C130 Hercules was a beast, a great cargo carrier and workhorse but not known for its manoeuvrability. The pilot, Flight Lieutenant Nathan MacDonald, was making a visual landing in tricky light with no horizon to guide him. The cloud base was low and the snow was blowing in a near whiteout. Where cloud met snow, the horizon vanished.

Normally such a flight would not have been attempted in such dangerous conditions in late April. But the call from McMurdo said one of their scientists was seriously ill and might not survive the upcoming winter. The Hercules had only an hour to load and turn around before darkness. If the plane did not take off on time then the aircraft and the ill scientist could be trapped on the ground for six months of winter darkness. The engines kept running in the extreme cold to ensure the Hercules remained operable as it was refuelled and the patient loaded. The aircraft flew back to Christchurch, New Zealand, seven hours away, but there was one odd development. Instead of rescuing one sick person, the Hercules crew was bringing back eleven people.

The dramatic rescue made headlines around the world and Flight Lieutenant MacDonald was later awarded a CBE — Commander of the British Empire — for his feat of flying. Such a heroic rescue of someone sick in the Antarctic was a good-news story and there should have been nothing to hide. But the authorities acted as if there was.

Journalists often encounter people in official positions who refuse to give out information because of legal restrictions or privacy considerations, or perhaps because they simply dislike the media or are secretive or paranoid by nature. A journalist should not of course assume that the authorities are always hiding something worth reporting when they won't talk. Likewise if they do talk but provide information that later proves inaccurate. Governments and corporations get things wrong and in an unfolding news story, early versions can turn out to be inaccurate.

But when inaccurate information is combined with unnecessary secrecy, then journalists will suspect that someone is deploying the tools of truth suppression. That is what happened in the Antarctic story, although the tool that was used turned out to be rather different than I expected. Many bureaucrats and even trained public relations officials don't seem to understand that if they act as if they are hiding something, journalists will simply get even more interested — and so it was after the rescue.

The first oddity was the number of those rescued. Initially the authorities said one person was airlifted for undisclosed medical reasons, then that became two, then four, and then eleven. When the flight landed at Christchurch, TV crews were kept well away from the plane and not allowed to film anyone. The media was told the ban was for 'political reasons'. The level of secrecy seemed well beyond the norm.

Various officials made contradictory statements. A spokesman for the US Antarctic program said that four of those on board were en route to Christchurch hospital in 'serious but stable conditions'. Media calls to the hospital revealed that one man was said to be a fireman named Dave Tamo, who said he had concussion after he had 'fallen over while carrying a computer and hit his head on a chair'. Another patient had bruises and a broken cheekbone and would not talk.

It seemed like the people at McMurdo were pretty accident-prone. Although it was a US base staffed by Americans, some of those brought off the ice were from other countries but in the secrecy the nationalities were not made known. A US spokesman later said seven of the eleven had been removed from the ice for undisclosed disciplinary reasons.

It emerged that there had been a strange request for salt. The request was received by the New Zealand Air Force, asking that their medics carry 'salt in their pockets' for the trip to Antarctic; later this was explained away by the US spokesman who said the base had 'run out of cooking salt'.

In the months following, media inquiries continued. The New Zealand Air Force warned a TV producer to stay away from the story, giving only unspecified security reasons. It was later learnt that four of those rescued were taken to the burns unit of a hospital in Denver, Colorado. Colorado was home to Raytheon Polar Services, a division of Raytheon Corp, a US$50 billion company which is a Pentagon defence contractor and which also designs and builds nuclear power plants. Raytheon employed nearly all the US workers in the Antarctic and in turn Raytheon was contracted by the National Science Foundation in the US, which was responsible for the US Antarctic mission.

The Antarctic Sun, an online paper that covered every tiny thing about life at the bases there, carried not a word about the rescue. The paper was owned by Raytheon. I was tipped off by a very reliable source that we should look into this story, that a serious accident had been followed by a cover-up. So with a researcher at TV3, New Zealand's commercial TV channel, we began an investigation.

Working under the cover of doing a story about life in the Antarctic, the researcher spoke to the navigator on the mission. After initially proving very helpful he started to clam up about more specific issues and started to 'forget' things that he had previously told us. One example was that after revealing a number of personal anecdotes about the civilian doctor who flew with them, he later claimed to be unable to recall the man's name. He also said he 'could not recall' the name of one of the critically ill men he rescued even though he had earlier said he had received an email from the man's grateful parents.

The New Zealand Air Force public relations officer said there were certain aspects of the rescue story that were sensitive and could not be discussed. Next, an internet site called Quickening News carried a strange story that referred to a nuclear accident in the Antarctic. The page was later removed and the Quickening News site could not be found in the weeks that followed. There was an internet link to the 'Daily event reports of nuclear accidents' at the US Government's Nuclear Regulatory Commission under the heading, 'Antarctic nuclear accident'. A search of the commission's site got the following message: 'the page you have requested no longer exists'.

Each one of these things could perhaps have been explained by unnecessary secrecy, misunderstanding or internet conspiracy weirdness but taken together, they seemed to add up to a classic cover-up of something we did not as yet know. I wrote a memo to my boss at TV3, Terence Taylor, with an ambitious request to go down to Antarctica to pursue the story. The memo is as good an example as any of how a journalist's mind works. We tend to have split personalities — sceptical of anything we are told but hopeful that at least some of it will be true and lead us to an interesting story.

After listing all the discrepancies and secrecy, I wrote in the memo:

Clearly Raytheon and the US government with the co-operation of the NZ government have gone to a great deal of time and trouble to prevent what happened from becoming public knowledge.

If it was a minor accident or fire, they would not have bothered to cover it up. A large fire at the British Antarctic research station in 2001 was extensively reported in the media, including the Raytheon-owned Antarctic Sun. One explanation is a nuclear accident ... the request for salt and the references at the nuclear regulatory commission point to this. Nuclear research is not barred by the Antarctic Treaty.

We should vigorously pursue this story as a potential world exclusive. Even if there is a more mundane explanation than nuclear they are hiding something. Also we should expect a strong reaction from Raytheon and the US government when they find out we are getting close to the story ... [US]$50 billion buys a lot of influence, and a lot of lawyers, and with government agencies involved, and the military, they will try and stop the story from ever coming out.

A few months later I was off to the ice. I was to produce a series of current affairs stories, with a cameraman and reporter, to try to get to the bottom of the rescue story.

Filming on the ice.

■ ■ ■

Antarctica is the driest, coldest continent, a truly beautiful place. Stand in front of, say, the Barnes Glacier and you are looking at one of the great wonders of the world. Stand there too long, even in the summer, and eventually your body will begin to shut down and you will freeze to death. Staff are scientists and technicians, firefighters and cooks, drivers and doctors. They may live in beauty but also in great isolation and that can lead to mental health problems. To stay sane, some of them drink to excess.

In between the actual work, there are wild parties and sexual hook-ups in strange places as privacy is an issue when everyone lives in such close proximity. Couples end up in cupboards or anywhere they can find to be alone, anywhere but outside. People drink huge quantities of beer, wine and spirits and even home brews. At one stage, people at the South Pole were drinking a home brew made in the lab using any rotting fruit that came to hand.

One man was found collapsed on the stairs, unconscious. Another vomited all over his workstation. A party at Scott Base, where the New Zealanders are, resulted in an American manager from McMurdo being sent home for sexual misconduct. Sometimes there are bizarre ceremonies such as a testicular measuring competition and examples of surprising incompetence like the complete breakdown of the water supply at the base.

Fights are regular and sometimes end up as bloody punch-ups involving several people. Such behaviour is mostly hidden from the outside world. Most stories are justifiably about the amazing work that goes on there and, of course, there is much more of that than there are drunken orgies and brawls. However, only rarely does a hint of the human cost of living in such an environment reach the public.

The Office of the Inspector General of the US Science Foundation conducted a health and safety audit of the American bases. Its remit included discipline, training the US Marshals who police their part of Antarctica and, stunningly, looking at whether breathalyzers should be used on staff on the ice to show if they were fit to work or under the influence.

National Science Foundation (NSF) officials said that the drinking had created major problems, 'unpredictable behaviour that has led to fights, indecent exposure, and employees arriving to work under the influence'[1]. Could such bad behaviour, the kind that would damage the image of the Antarctic missions, be a reason why governments were so keen to cover up details of the rescue flight that I had investigated?

Sources later told me there could have been innocent explanations for the request for salt — far removed from a nuclear accident. McMurdo frequently ran out of basics and ordered things to be brought in on the next available flight. We learnt that the numbers of people going on medevac flights sometimes changed at the last minute. People hearing a flight was available would simply quit their jobs and turn up to get on the plane. They had had enough and wanted to go home. It was not necessarily suspicious.

In his book *Big Dead Place*, former Antarctic worker Nicholas Johnson described some of the fights:

> *An ironworker threw a drink in the face of a bartender who then threw the ironworker on the floor. The ironworker, who had recently attacked someone with a pool cue, was certain to go out on the*

plane. A painter who was wrestling with the Kiwis over at Scott Base
crashed his face into the corner of a table and would be flown out for
reconstructive surgery. Two guys at the bar had a heated argument
over who had been to Black Island more times. One threw a bottle at
the other, cutting his hand.[2]

These could have been among the large group who were in the RNZAF Hercules that night, in which case it was simply a case of an inept cover-up of a minor matter sparking theories of something much more significant. It wouldn't be the first time I had examined a story that appeared to be major but turned out rather different. It's one of the perils of investigative reporting — you can spend weeks or months on a story that falls away or you simply never get answers to your questions.

I could not, however, get an explanation as to why four of those rescued had ended up in a burns unit when there was no report of any fire or accident involving chemicals. I was trying to develop sources at the hospital and at Raytheon to give me more details when my attention was diverted by another Antarctic mystery. A scientist had been found dead at South Pole Station, in circumstances that suggested foul play.

At 90° South, the pole flags are as ubiquitous as snow and ice. Yet out of the hundreds on station, sixteen specific flags are the most coveted souvenirs of a South Pole winter. At sunset once each year, the thirteen national flags from the poles are raffled off amongst the general population. The three flags at the main entrance — of the United States, the National Science Foundation, and the US Antarctic Program — are then awarded to deserving workers. A break in this tradition occurred in 2014, when the three entrance flags were left outdoors.

Darkness gradually descended, escorted by plummeting temperatures and howling storms. The wind feasted on each flag still flying. The flags needed replacing. A couple of the workers knew just what to do when one of the new flags could not be attached. They found a replacement. It was six months before the sun's ascension revealed the pirate flag flying over the South Pole. The pirate symbol was apt. Antarctica is a wild place where dozens of countries have laid claim to parts of the ice but none rules. The continent is governed by the Antarctic Treaty. It does not stop any country claiming sovereignty but it doesn't support such claims either. There is no overall body in charge of the continent, no ice-wide police force. Who, for instance, would be responsible for investigating a possible murder?

■ ■ ■

South Pole Station — Amundsen–Scott Station to give it its correct name — is a US base, the only base at the pole. It sits on a plateau some 3000 metres (9300 feet) above sea level and has six months of 24-hour a day sunshine followed by six months of total darkness. It sits on 3 kilometres (1¾ miles) of ice and below that there is water. The ice is moving all the time beneath the station — that movement means the South Pole itself moves 10 metres (11 yards) each year. In winter, the temperatures can drop to –73 °C (–98 °F). It houses about 200 people in the summer months and those wintering over usually number around 50. Most of the science work is astronomy — the low temperatures and dryness of the air make it a perfect setting for experiments.

Rodney David Marks, an Australian astrophysicist, was working on such experiments when he died at the station on 12 May 2000. Marks was born in Geelong in the state of Victoria and was educated in Melbourne and Sydney, where he got his PhD from the University of New South Wales. He had wintered over at the South Pole Station previously and had returned to work on a research project for the University of Chicago, the Antarctic Submillimeter Telescope and Remote Observatory. He was in a relationship with a maintenance worker who was wintering over with him.

On 11 May Marks became unwell while walking between the remote observatory and the base. He became increasingly sick over a 36-hour period, during which he made three visits to the base doctor. His condition could not be diagnosed and he died a day later. He was only 32 years old but people at the base nevertheless assumed he had died of natural causes. Because it was winter, his body could not be removed so it was kept at the base for six months until flights resumed with the arrival of the Antarctic spring in November, when it was flown to Christchurch, the air gateway to the Antarctic, in the South Island of New Zealand.

There was a post mortem and the result was unexpected. Marks had not died of natural causes. The coroner found significant levels of methanol in his body but was unable to establish how the poison got there. Marks had died at an American base but his body was now in New Zealand. A New Zealand police investigation got underway, led by then Detective Senior Sergeant Grant Wormald, an experienced investigator who later rose to become deputy director of the organized and financial crime agency. The Marks inquiry was to be one of the most frustrating of his career, as US authorities repeatedly stonewalled his attempts to review the facts and interview witnesses.

Christchurch was seven hours' flying time from Scott and McMurdo, about 4000 kilometres (2500 miles). South Pole Station was a further 1360 kilometres (850 miles) south. The distance was already a huge issue for the investigators and their problems were compounded by the lack of co-operation. What, if anything, were the Americans trying to hide? Police took the view that it was highly unlikely that Marks had knowingly ingested the methanol either in a suicide attempt or some bizarre self-experiment.

They focused on three possibilities: that he was murdered, was the victim of a prank gone wrong or of an act of criminal negligence such as mislabelling chemicals. Detectives began by trying to obtain a list of all those working at the station the day Marks died. It seemed a simple task but US authorities refused to help. At one stage, police were reduced to searching on the internet for clues as to who had been down there.

When they did finally find a staff list they had to painstakingly negotiate the details of a questionnaire to be sent to these staff who were potential witnesses to a murder or other criminal act. The questionnaire was finally agreed with the questions approved by the National Science Foundation. In no other police inquiry would potential witnesses be given the questions in advance. In any event, only thirteen out of 49 people bothered to reply.

'I suspect there have been people who have thought twice about making contact with us on the basis of their future employment situation,' Detective Senior Sergeant Wormald told one newspaper. Police believed a full investigation into the events leading to Marks's death had been carried out by the US agencies but they were refused access to the results of that investigation. 'It is impossible to say how far that investigation went or to what end,' Wormald told the inquest. Coroner Richard McElrea in his findings highlighted the difficulties in getting help from the National Science Foundation and Raytheon Polar Services.

Marks's family were in despair at the lack of co-operation. His father Paul complained there had been no contact from either Raytheon or the NSF. He did not understand why it was proving so difficult to get answers out of them. 'For heaven's sake, a man has died in your care. Why wouldn't you help the police?' Marks was known to be a heavy drinker and he suffered from Tourette's syndrome; colleagues alleged that he drank to mask the symptoms. But that was not unusual in a community of serious drinkers. He was not known for angry outbursts nor did he get into fights. He was very popular with his fellow scientists.

A colleague described him to one journalist as a brilliant and witty man who drank to excess 'on occasion'. The post mortem showed he had needle marks on his arms but there were no illegal drugs in his body. Police were sceptical over one suggestion that he distilled his own booze and accidentally poisoned himself. Alcohol was freely available on base although some still preferred to brew their own. In any case, Marks was the sort of person who would have known the dangers of making your own spirits. Suicide seemed the least likely reason, as he appeared happy; he was in a close relationship and was active in his work and social life. His experiments were going well and he was working towards publication of a significant piece of academic work. He had no financial worries.

Detective Senior Sergeant Wormald discovered that an NSF doctor had recommended an investigation in the immediate aftermath of the death: 'When an individual aged 32 years dies unexpectedly, the matter warrants a homicide investigation.' But instead of evidence being gathered, South Pole staff were allowed to clean Marks's room, disposing as rubbish any potential evidence. Staff at the station could have been made available for interviews after they left the base because they all had to land back in Christchurch before dispersing around the world, but that was not done. The foundation did nothing to halt the 49 people leaving Antarctica from disappearing across the world without being interviewed after landing in New Zealand.

Not only were the Americans not helping, they were exerting diplomatic pressure behind the scenes. At one stage the US State Department contacted the New Zealand Ministry of Foreign Affairs and Trade in Wellington to try to find out why the Kiwi detective was being so persistent in his inquiries.

■ ■ ■

The Marks file remains open. He died of methanol poisoning but there has been no finding as to why. Suicide has been ruled out — the coroner could find no evidence of murder, either. We may never know why Marks died, just as the reason why four people rescued from the ice ended up in a burns unit in hospital also remains a mystery.

The responses to the death and the rescue mission have some of the hallmarks of a cover-up and predictably both have led to other conspiracy theories. But there is a simpler explanation: the

US government, the NSF and Raytheon did not want either story examined too closely for fear of what it might reveal about life in Antarctica. In the Marks case, some witnesses testified that cannabis was grown and that a stash of marijuana was found at one of the base's large telescopes. Both the death and the rescue could have shone a spotlight on drugs, binge drinking, fights and rampant sex — but this is not the pristine image of life on the ice that they want to project.

So the authorities prevented a proper murder inquiry and obscured details of the rescue to stop too many awkward questions being asked. They would have not been able to do so if the incidents had happened in a more accessible place. If either incident had happened in any city or town in the West, the media would have descended en masse, tracking down interviewees and bombarding the authorities with questions. There would have been lots of cameras and press conferences, and pressure to release more information.

But here, the classic truth-prevention tool of distance was used to keep police, journalists and family members at bay. The obstruction and secrecy has denied the Marks family answers they are entitled to. They do not believe they will ever know how their son was poisoned. The array of flags at South Pole Station now includes one that does not represent just a nation but also a man — Rodney David Marks, the only man ever to die at the station. Unlike the others, the Australian flag stays out all winter as a tribute to him. Each year, as the ice moves, the flag gets further and further away from the base. Eventually it will disappear.

South Pole Station where Marks died.

Flags around the pole.

THE TRUTH-BLOCKING VALUE OF DISTANCE

We live in an interconnected, wired-up world where it's popular to talk about the death of distance. But distance still counts in journalism. The further you are from easy access for television crews, the more likely you are to be able to hide your crimes. Any smart dictator knows that if you are going to commit a massacre, you need to keep the cameras away. Otherwise, we might start paying attention.

Critics of the media often ask why the appalling atrocities committed over decades in the Congo have not been as well reported as, say, the civil war in Syria. Owen Jones, writing in *The Guardian*, said:

> Some lives matter more than others: the hierarchy of death, they call it. The millions killed, maimed and traumatised in the Democratic Republic of Congo are surely at the bottom of this macabre pile. The country was the site of the deadliest war since the fall of Adolf Hitler, and yet I doubt most people in the West are even aware of it. No heart-wrenching exclusives at the top of news bulletins; no mounting calls for western militaries to 'do something'. [3]

The tragedy of the Congo has indeed not received the coverage it deserved: millions dead, mass rapes, starvation, cannibalism, armed groups rampaging around the country. But a more basic explanation is distance. It is a difficult country to get to, and it is even more difficult — and dangerous — to travel into. It is 2.3 million square kilometres (890,000 square miles), in size: bigger than Spain, France, Germany, Sweden and Norway put together, and lacking in infrastructure and connections to the outside world.

The best reporting comes from being at the scene of the crime, the disaster or other newsworthy event. But cutbacks in newsroom budgets mean that trips to remote areas, jungle or ice or rainforests, are now rare. Reporters doing four stories a day for print or TV as well as online often can't even get out of the office, never mind contemplating travelling for days or weeks to a remote area to cover a story.

Brave journalists can and do cover the Congo but its remoteness, like that of Antarctica, means that events there that should be reported often are not and, in many cases, the reporting is second-hand, written at a desk far away. Such reporting often has to rely on official sources that may be just as interested in disguising things as disclosing them. Distance still counts.

8.

From the toolbox: Official secrets and other means of suppression

HOW TO AVOID A GOVERNMENT STOPPING YOUR BOOK BEING PUBLISHED

IN THE NEWS, 18 JANUARY 2018

LeBron James to become seventh NBA
    player to reach 30,000 points
Dow Jones finishes above 26,000 for first time
President Trump hands out Fake News awards
Best-selling action author Andy McNab
    launches petition to force council
    to house homeless ex-SAS man

The frozen smile on the face of the legendary special forces soldier said it all. Andy McNab, holder of the Distinguished Conduct Medal and the Military Medal, author of *Bravo Two Zero*, one of the best-selling war books of all time, who had killed men in combat, did not like the question he had just been asked. We were in the middle of a TV interview for a program I was producing on the SAS.

McNab had been captured while on a patrol behind enemy lines in Iraq and tortured, according to his book. His teeth had been smashed while he was being beaten and his interrogator had offered him the assistance of a dentist. In our interview, he described the ordeal in grim detail:

Q. You also suffered didn't you a lot of damage to your teeth, and they took you to see a dentist?

A. Yeah, certainly in the beginning getting caught … the soldiers initially had their bit with the capture and then the officers would take over and we were both sat on chairs in one of the offices, so it would start with a poke, then it would be a punch, then it would be a kick, then you'd go on the floor, and what I got on my left hand side [was] my molars were split into segments, into quarters in fact, split down the sides and bit hanging out, and one of them, one of the quarters was still in and um I went to interrogation and it was the same interrogator in fact, the old one, said well you know again this thing we're not barbaric, we know that you've got teeth damage, and we have a dentist who's worked in London, in fact spent nine years in London, and the frustrating thing you can't see anything, cos you're always blindfolded, and this character came in who was all very sort of very fast talking, and yeah there's not problems. I've worked nine years in the UK, and what he done he actually pulled it out with a pair of pliers.

Q. You couldn't see what was happening, you assumed he was going to fix your teeth?

A. Well yeah it was just a matter of well hopefully he will but let's just wait and see. It was just that that — just accepting it really, there wasn't so much — well there wasn't nothing you could do, physically there was nothing you could do, because they controlled you physically, the whole thing and the whole aim of surviving that situation what I'd learned before that experience and which is certainly my experience endorses is actually accepting what physically goes on, but mentally you're keeping that mental integrity, and just hope that you survive, get through the other side.

Q. He pulled out one of your molars or what was left?

A. With a pair of pliers yeah. It was very much like the burn, there was just lots of screaming and your body sort of goes tall, and then the rhetoric from the interrogator you know, do you really think we're gonna help you, you know you're not helping us, and then the interrogation starts.

Q. Did you pass out?

A. No, not at that stage, about ten minutes later yeah. Not at that stage cos it was that shock that very sort of — very painful shock.

The teeth torture story was one of the most gripping passages in *Bravo Two Zero*. Millions of people had read it — and he had repeated the story in a number of interviews. But we had just referred him to a photo taken on his release from captivity in Baghdad. In the photo he was smiling and he displayed a perfect set of white teeth. He was smiling at us now, but his eyes told a different story. *So that's what they mean when they say if looks could kill*, I thought.

Andy McNab (real name: Steven Billy Mitchell) was the patrol leader and his book was one of two bestsellers about the mission behind Iraqi lines in the first Gulf War. The other was *The One That Got Away* by Chris Ryan, the alias of Chris Armstrong. *Bravo Two Zero* was a tale of heroism and survival against the odds and did wonders for the reputation of the SAS. It had all the drama and action of a Hollywood movie and it was turned into a television mini-series. There is a third Bravo Two Zero book, *Soldier Five*, which is less well known.

The British government spent millions of pounds of taxpayers' money in court battles to stop another SAS man, who went by the alias of Mike Coburn, talking or writing about the mission despite it being one of the most widely publicized military operations of all time. It was truth suppression on a grand scale, using one of the oldest tools available: the sledgehammer of official secrets and confidentiality contracts. The government lost most of the court battles but that did not deter them. They kept pursuing Coburn, year after year, deploying lawyer after lawyer, trying to wear him down.

The unequitable treatment of the soldiers has had long-term consequences. McNab and Ryan are now famous authors. Coburn lives in obscurity, working as a security consultant. Many other books by SAS men have been published since, without attracting the massive deployment of legal and bureaucratic resources brought to bear against Coburn. I wanted to find out why Coburn had been singled out and what really happened on the mission.

In *Bravo Two Zero*, McNab refers to another member of the patrol who was captured and interrogated by the Iraqis, known as Mark the

Kiwi. Assuming him to be a New Zealander, I set out to find him for part of a New Zealand television program. We tracked down McNab, who gave us an interview in London. He was what people in the television industry call 'good talent'. He was confident, at ease on camera, a born storyteller and he was happy to co-operate with our story.

McNab promised to contact Mark the Kiwi on our behalf and gave us some details about him, saying he was part Māori. Later I realized that what details he gave us about 'Mark' seemed to be designed to put us off the scent, so we would never find him. I did eventually find Mark the Kiwi and met him at the Empire Hotel in Auckland. He was definitely not part Māori, and other things McNab told me about him were clearly not true. He was angry about the books by McNab and Ryan and was thinking about writing a book of his own, under the pen name Mike Coburn. (Note: I have chosen not to reveal Coburn's real identity here. It has to my knowledge not been publicly disclosed, even in court documents, unlike the real names of McNab and Ryan.) It was clear that McNab and Coburn, former brothers in arms, were now on opposite sides.

McNab and Coburn had two things in common: they were both orphans and both good soldiers. McNab, according to his biography, was found abandoned on the steps of Guy's Hospital in Southwark in a Harrods shopping bag. He was brought up in Peckham, with his adoptive family. He did not do well in school, dropped out and worked at odd jobs, and was involved in some petty crime. He was arrested for burglary but not sent to prison. He tried to become an army pilot but failed the entry test. He finally enlisted in the army, in the Royal Green Jackets, at age sixteen. After serving in Northern Ireland and earning the Military Medal for his actions during a gun battle with IRA men in South Armagh, he joined the SAS in 1984.

Coburn was born in Auckland at National Women's Hospital and was adopted at birth by a couple who had emigrated from Britain after World War II. His adopted father was an ex-RAF bomber navigator who joined the New Zealand Air Force. His mother was in the New Zealand Army nursing corps. He went to Mount Albert Grammar, widely considered to be one of Auckland's best schools, where he excelled at rugby and history. Aged nineteen, he passed selection for the New Zealand Special Air Service but in search of a new challenge he went to the UK and passed another brutal selection course to join the British SAS. He joined B Squadron just in time to join the patrol which was given the call sign Bravo Two Zero.

In interviews, McNab was a fast talker. Coburn was quieter and chose his words carefully. The two men had fought alongside each other and been captured together. But their accounts of the mission could not have differed more.[1] They were together when they came under fire, and Coburn was hit in the leg and arm. In McNab's account: 'There was certainly no screaming and no noise coming from him. So as far as I was concerned he was dead as soon as they opened fire. Thankfully, he's not lying there dying because you know you tend to hear that people will make sure you know that they're alive.'

In Coburn's account: 'This huge wave of nausea went over me. I mean really intense … but there wasn't any pain and another round went off through my arm and then the pain sort of came along and I started screaming. I was screaming my head off.' McNab kept going, leaving the New Zealander in the hands of the Iraqis. Later, McNab himself was captured. They were interrogated for six weeks. McNab said when he was released he had nerve damage to both hands, a dislocated shoulder, kidney and liver damage, hepatitis and the smashed teeth.

Coburn: 'I certainly know that he was beaten. Now whether he was tortured to the extent that he said he was … when we were released in Baghdad together he certainly made no comment of that and I certainly didn't see any evidence of the fact.'

McNab: 'What happened is that I got my teeth knocked out. I got burnt. I got whipped. I got hit by the four-by-two and hit with metallic balls.'

When I interviewed McNab, I asked: 'Coburn says you had all your teeth intact when he saw you at the time of your release?'

McNab: 'Well that's very strange … the fact is that they were smashed in the back and that's why I'm still getting them sorted out two weeks ago.'

Coburn: 'I think McNab's book is, the best way to put it is it doesn't do anybody any harm but what he does is he does certainly elevate his position in his role perhaps more than it should be. That was for the purposes of selling his book … he's the one who has to take stock of that and he's the one who has to live with that.'

The two men no longer spoke. They used to go to Gulf War POW reunions together but according to Coburn, McNab was no longer invited to them 'by mutual agreement of everybody, which is not just the SAS guys; it's with the Tornado pilots and navigators as well. It is a question over an unpaid hotel bill which he refused to front up for.' McNab made a lot of money from his books but according to Coburn the unpaid bill was for less than £50.

HOW DO YOU KNOW WHEN INTERVIEWEES ARE TELLING THE TRUTH?

This is the question I am most often asked by students when I talk to them about investigative reporting.

The golden rule in journalism is to attribute, that is to quote the person you have interviewed in your story, thus making them responsible for what they say. Of course this rule does not work when you are quoting sources whom you have agreed not to identify, for reasons of their personal safety or because they face prosecution if they are discovered talking to you.

You can check what they say with other sources and against what is already known about the story. If what they are telling you contradicts that, it doesn't mean they are lying or mistaken. They could simply have better information, or more direct knowledge, or a different point of view.

It is important to consider motive, such as what is behind this person telling you a secret? Whistleblowers can be acting out of a genuine sense of public spirit; they are outraged by something a government or corporation has done and they want people to know about it. They could be trying to do down someone they don't like, to damage their reputation. Perhaps they have a grievance because they were denied a promotion, not paid what they think they deserve or because their work is not getting enough respect. It is clear that Peter Wright of *Spycatcher* fame would not have written his book if the UK government had paid him a decent pension.

Sometimes the motive is solely greed because they want to be paid for their story. (I have never paid an interviewee, although I have sometimes reimbursed legitimate expenses for such things as travel.) Major stories have come from whistleblowers acting out of greed or malice; people acting from the purest of motives have got it wrong. Descriptions of the same event can be radically different but not necessarily because someone is trying to deceive you.

McNab and Coburn gave completely different accounts of the moment Coburn was shot but in the heat of battle, with adrenaline taking over, it is possible that they simply heard and saw different things. Always be sceptical of blow-by-blow accounts of battles. Soldiers are not dispassionately recording what is happening — they are trying to stay alive. The same goes for any reporters at the scene, or civilians, and for anyone caught up in a major disaster.

So how do you tell that an interviewee is telling the truth? You can judge some things by experience. If someone starts threatening you over a question you have asked them — I have been told 'we know where you live' a surprising number of times — they are usually hiding something. Ditto for an instant threat to sue you.

But some people have been trained to keep calm and lie with great fluency, and not just politicians. Politicians will lie of course, if they have to, but they are afraid of being caught in the lie so they will often simply change the question. 'I think what you are really trying to ask me is this.' 'I think the question the public really want to ask is this.' 'I think what you really mean is this.' Then they will give the answer they want; just not the answer to the question they were asked.

I have been lied to by some of the best. Every journalist has met outright fraudsters and they are usually good liars. Intelligence officers can be expert deceivers and special forces soldiers, too, are used to operating under false identities. They have to be convincing because their life depends on it.

Good reporters are aware of their limitations. You can cross-check, use instinct and judgment born of experience. But the honest answer is that of course you can't always tell if the person you are interviewing is telling the truth. The tendency has been for journalists and media organizations to pretend they are more accurate and more knowledgeable than they are. We are far better off being honest with the public about the limitations of our craft. Good journalists seek the truth — but they don't always find it. Journalism is not a science. There is a reason it has been called 'the first rough draft of history', with the emphasis on the rough.

The UK government clearly did not care about the differing accounts of battle in the books, even less that the patrol members had fallen out, or who did or did not settle a hotel bill for £50. So why did they allow McNab and Ryan's books to be published while going after Coburn?

They did not have the weapon of the confidentiality contract to go after the first two but they had other tools they could have used against the books. Special forces missions are secret, after all. It was widely recognized within both the SAS and the SBS, the Special Boat Service, that they were bound by a code of silence. But court documents later showed that Britain's Ministry of Defence was happy to assist McNab with his book. He got the thumbs up; Coburn got years of legal bills.

The eight-member Bravo Two Zero patrol was dropped behind Iraqi lines in the first Gulf War. The patrol was compromised. Three men died, four were captured and one — Ryan/Armstrong — escaped to Syria. McNab and Ryan's books are tales of daring; they have the elements of a boys' own adventure. The courage described is real even if some of the descriptions have been challenged. McNab was awarded the DCM, the Distinguished Conduct Medal, after the mission.

Coburn's book is very different. He describes the patrol as a disaster, he damns the regiment's officers and their methods. Coburn accused the SAS command — including the officer who later became director of UK Special Forces and who tried to stop his book being published — of abandoning the men.

'You have a thing called a guardnet, which means you can communicate directly with your squadron, and that's a fixed frequency. We managed to get through to say that we were in the shit and we needed help. Unfortunately it was ignored.' It later emerged that the SAS command had decided a rescue mission was too dangerous. It was part of the SAS ethos that, no matter how much difficulty a patrol got into, the regiment would always take urgent steps to get it out, regardless of where it was. In the case of Bravo Two Zero, however, it appeared that the need to send more men and aircraft in search of Iraqi Scud missiles was deemed more important than the plight of the patrol.

Coburn laid the blame for the deaths of his three comrades squarely at the door of the SAS regimental hierarchy. Moreover, he said that in the post-mission debriefing in Hereford, the commanding officer admitted that aspects of the regimental support system had not functioned well, and in some cases not at all. 'Shocking among his revelations to us was the statement that he had decided not to court-martial the surviving members of the patrol. The reference to court martial was a shock. It seemed incredible after all we had been through. There was no justification for even mentioning it and it came completely out of the blue …' (To this day, Coburn has no idea why a court martial should have been mentioned.)

Coburn also complained about equipment failures during the mission. The risks involved in special forces work was something soldiers prepared for, he said, but incompetence was something he did not expect. 'Being told we were expendable after the fact only served to compound the betrayal of trust.'

McNab and Coburn, in our interviews, had strikingly different views of the commanders.

McNab:

At the end of the day a commanding officer gets paid a vast amount of money to sit there and think I've got eight men on the ground, I don't know what's happened to them. I don't know if they are alive or dead, do I send one of our aircraft in, a helicopter with a crew and another eight men, I don't know. Actually he made the right choice because the aircraft would have been shot down because there was far too much enemy activity in the area … personally I would have liked an aircraft coming in but you are paid to be a soldier and that's the decision he made and I stick by that.

Coburn:

That's fine if you know that, if they tell you that beforehand then you can get that mindset into your head and make your own contingencies for that. But you know that was never ever made clear to us before we went out. I was disgusted. I certainly felt ... that the hierarchy of the regiment during the Gulf War let a lot of the guys down.

SAS men all have to sign lifetime confidentiality agreements that override many of their basic rights as citizens. Coburn had to sign — the contracts were introduced after the McNab book came out. The contracts bar them, even after they leave the SAS, from doing what army officers have done for centuries: making money from their memoirs.

Indeed the first book to refer to the Bravo Two Zero patrol, *Storm Command*, was written by a senior officer, General Sir Peter de la Billière. The book disclosed many details including Ryan's escape on foot across the desert into Syria. The Ministry of Defence took no action to prevent its publication. The confidentiality contracts were introduced because the government became concerned at the prospect of other special forces soldiers writing books or taking part in TV programs.

In particular, they were alarmed by the prospect of disclosures about operations in Northern Ireland where SAS soldiers were at the forefront of the long and brutal campaign to defeat the paramilitaries of the IRA. SAS soldiers working undercover frequently clashed with IRA gunmen — many of the IRA men ended up dead. Coburn had worked in Northern Ireland after Bravo Two Zero, although no details were disclosed in his book. The new contracts were draconian, to say the least.

Confidentiality contract

Between the MOD and [full name]

In consideration of me being given a continued posting in the United Kingdom Special Forces ... by the MOD I hereby give the solemn undertaking binding me for the rest of my life.

I will not disclose without express prior permission in writing from MOD any information, document or other article relating to the work of or in support of the United Kingdom Special Forces which is or has been in my possession by virtue of my position as a member of any of those forces

I will not make any statement without express prior authority in writing from MOD which purports to be a disclosure of such information as is referred to in paragraph 1 above or is intended to be taken, or might reasonably be taken, by those to whom it is addressed as being such a disclosure

I will assign to MOD all rights accruing to me and arising out of, or in connection with, any disclosure or statement in breach of paragraph 1 or 2 above

I will bring immediately to the notice of MOD any occasion on which a person invited me to breach this contract.

The sweeping nature of this type of contract was later summed up by Justice Salmon in the New Zealand High Court. He said it allowed the Ministry of Defence in the UK to impose a lifelong ban 'of any information, no matter how innocuous or lacking in sensitivity or confidentiality' relating to the work of special forces.

Coburn was in the US when he was told about the contracts and verbally ordered to sign by the regiment's commanding officer. Back in London, he was verbally ordered to sign by his immediate superior, a senior sergeant. Then at the SAS base in Hereford he was given another verbal order to sign. Coburn protested throughout. He was not allowed to study a copy in advance and neither was he allowed to keep a copy after signature. Permission to show it to a lawyer was denied. Coburn was told that if he refused to sign he would be 'returned to unit', meaning he would be transferred out of the SAS, losing his status and the special pay that went with it. The pay cut would be in the region of 40 per cent — at least £20,000 a year. Coburn finally signed the contract under protest and duress.

Such contracts can be used to protect genuine secrets. But no special forces soldier I have ever met — and I have interviewed more than twenty — would seek to disclose anything that would compromise or risk the lives of their fellow soldiers. They never talk about upcoming missions, or missions that are still a secret, or weapons and tactics that are not already public knowledge. The contracts are, however, like the Official Secrets Act, very useful in enforcing cover-ups and protecting past operations from public scrutiny.

It stops soldiers ever revealing details of special forces blunders. If they are involved in an operation that ends up as a shambles, they can never make the truth known. They cannot complain if they are abandoned by their commanders and left to die when they get into difficulties. They cannot question the decision making of politicians and senior officers, even over missions that are historical.

Coburn was unhappy with his treatment and finally left the SAS. He decided to write the book with fellow patrol member Mal Macgown, an Australian. Their principal goal was to set the record straight as they were particularly upset by the way in which the death of one of their fellow soldiers, Sergeant Vince Phillips, had been portrayed. Phillips, the second in command, had died of hypothermia while fleeing the Iraqis. Coburn and Macgown believed that Phillips had been unfairly treated in Ryan's book, and made a scapegoat for the failure of the mission.

Phillips, like the other dead men — troopers Bob Consilgio and Steven Lane — were identified in the books by their real names. McNab and Ryan's decision to use pseudonyms while identifying the dead soldiers had also caused anger in the regiment. Coburn and Macgown had no intention of revealing any secrets. They were writing about a mission that had received worldwide publicity in books and films. They submitted their manuscript to the Ministry of Defence in London.

■ ■ ■

Months after we first met in Auckland we travelled to Hereford to meet Coburn and his Welsh wife Sue, who was an aerobics instructor, at their home. Coburn had left the SAS and joined the world of security and bodyguard work in what former special forces soldiers call 'the circuit'. He worked part of each month at an oil installation in North Africa. We took him to do some filming up in the Welsh national park of Brecon Beacons, where SAS men train in brutal marches and escape and evasion exercises. It was a cold and bleak place but Coburn was in his element and happily jogged and sprinted up and down hills while the camera rolled.

He agreed to be interviewed for Television New Zealand's *Assignment*, on the understanding he would discuss matters that were already in the public domain. He courageously agreed to appear on camera without any disguise — even though his work undercover in

Northern Ireland still made him a potential target for the IRA or one of its splinter groups. It would be a world first.

Once again, I was relying on the British obsession with secrecy not being supported by judges and the public in New Zealand and that the confidentiality contract would not be enforceable in another jurisdiction. For a start, Coburn was a New Zealand citizen and what he had been forced to sign was clearly in breach of the New Zealand Bill of Rights. 'Mark the Kiwi' had the right to be treated as a Kiwi. And the story was clearly in the public interest. The British government, however, was determined to make an example of Coburn to discourage others. What followed was a frightening demonstration of the power of a government to bring pressure to bear on an individual. It was to be a one-sided fight.

MONEY AND LAWYERS ARE THE BEST FORM OF DEFENCE

An injunction is a favourite weapon of governments and corporations to prevent inconvenient truths coming out. It is issued in advance of a story to prevent it being published or broadcast and it is expensive and time-consuming to fight. The legal bills can be huge — millions of dollars or pounds — and if you lose, you are liable for costs. There is often no accountability for the taxpayers' money that is spent by governments or shareholders' money spent by corporations to attack the media. But there can be dire consequences for cash-strapped media companies or publishers.

The injunction is a form of prior restraint — that is, attacking a story in the courts *before* it comes out. The United States has excellent protections for freedom of the press enshrined in the First Amendment and does not allow prior restraint.

The other major legal threat is to be sued for libel — another costly business. In most court cases you are innocent until proven guilty but in a libel case the opposite applies. A journalist or publisher must prove innocence by showing the story is true and in the public interest. If the jury or judge finds against you, huge damages can be awarded. Public distrust of the media and the dubious activities of tabloids, gossip columnists and dodgy online sites means juries can be predisposed to believe the worst of reporters, even those doing serious journalism in the public interest.

Again, the United States has more protections for investigative reporting. In the US, public figures can only sue if the media publish things knowing them to be false. If journalists are acting maliciously, in other words. An injunction usually begins with a threatening letter from a lawyer:

Bell Gully Buddle Weir
IBM Centre
171 Featherston Street
Wellington New Zealand
PO Box 1291 Wellington

Telephone 64-4-473 7777
Facsimile 64-4-473 3845
DX: SX11164
Internet Home Page:
http://www.bgbw.co.nz

Bell Gully

BARRISTERS AND SOLICITORS

The General Counsel
Television New Zealand Limited
Television Centre
AUCKLAND

Our ref   C F Finlayson
Direct Dial 64-4-495 7980
Email   christopher.finlayson@bellgully.co.nz

8 October 1998

BY FACSIMILE 9-375 0900

Dear Sir

MIKE COBURN

We act for the British Government.

It has come to our attention late this morning that Television New Zealand has prepared a documentary on the abovenamed who was trained as an SAS soldier in New Zealand and then subsequently served in UK Special Forces. We have also been informed that it is the intention of TVNZ to broadcast the documentary, if not on tonight's Assignment programme then in the very near future.

In October 1996, Mr Coburn signed a confidentiality contract with the Secretary of State for Defence in the United Kingdom in which he undertook to keep confidential all aspects of his period of service with the UK Special Forces. Since his discharge from UK Special Forces, it has come to the attention of the British Government that he is intending to publish a book on his experiences in UK Special Forces. Any attempt to do so would constitute a breach of his contract with Secretary of State for Defence and constitute a breach of confidence.

The purpose of this letter is to advise you of this fact and to seek an undertaking from you that no material derived from Mr Coburn relating to his employment by, activities in, or knowledge of the UK Special Forces will be broadcast by TVNZ.

If you fail or refuse to comply with this request, we are under instructions to proceed to seek orders against TVNZ. Could we please have your response by 3.30pm?

Would you please acknowledge receipt of this letter?

Yours faithfully

C. F. Finlayson

BELL GULLY BUDDLE WEIR
C F Finlayson
Partner

Another day, another injunction.

197

IBM Centre
171 Featherston Street
P O Box 1291
Wellington New Zealand

Telephone 64 4 473 7777
Facsimile 64 4 473 3845
www.bellgully.com
DX SX11164

By facsimile 09 366 5999

The Chief Executive
Television 3
Auckland

Contact · C F Finlayson
Direct line 64 4 915 6980
Mobile 021 892118
Email christopher.finlayson@bellgully.com
Matter no. 01-274-0408

5 September 2002

Dear Sir

20/20 - SUNDAY, 8 SEPTEMBER

We act for the British Ministry of Defence which has instructed us to write to you about a programme which is going to be broadcast on TV3's 20/20 series on Sunday, 8 September. Evidently the programme concerns activities in Afghanistan undertaken by NZSAS. The producer is Stephen Davis.

The British Ministry of Defence has been told by the New Zealand Ministry of Defence (NZMOD) that in the course of Mr Davis' research, he may have been given the name of a New Zealander who was once a member of NZSAS but is now a member of UK Special Forces (UKSF). Apparently the programme will refer to this soldier although Mr Davis has apparently assured a representative of NZMOD that the soldier will not be named but will be given a letter indicator.

The British Ministry of Defence is concerned lest the soldier be named or other information relating to him be released into the public domain that could lead to his, or any other member of UKSF's identity, becoming known. It is imperative that not only the name of the soldier not be disclosed but that nothing be said which could lead to his identity becoming known. Moreover it is essential that there be nothing said in the programme which could disclose the identities of any other member of UKSF.

Accordingly, we would be grateful if you could give us an assurance that no information about UKSF will be disclosed in the forthcoming programme. We would also be grateful if, as a matter of urgency, a copy of the proposed programme could be made available so that it could be viewed by us. We would be prepared to make arrangements to see the programme either later today or tomorrow.

Because of the urgency of the matter, could you please contact our Mr Finlayson as soon as possible.

Yours faithfully
Bell Gully

C F Finlayson
Partner

The attempt to tell his story put an immense strain on the Coburns, both Mike and Sue. Sue had met Mike at a Hereford nightclub. She thought he was funny and she liked his Kiwi accent. Women travelled from all over the world to Hereford in the hope of meeting an SAS man, she told us. 'The place was full of very eligible bachelors. They were super-fit, ruggedly handsome and really nice people.'

But Sue had never been interested in army guys. Mike told her he was a rugby player but she knew the man with him was a regiment man. Mike and Sue dated a few times then Coburn disappeared. The next time she saw him he was on crutches, his foot smashed by a bullet during the Bravo Two Zero mission. Their relationship developed and they were married the following year in the army chapel in what most people might think an unusual ceremony. Coburn was an SAS man so he was not allowed to be married in uniform and the couple were not allowed to photograph their wedding. The photos were taken later in a studio. The regiment also had to give permission before they could move in together.

Being married to a special forces soldier or one who is on 'the circuit' is tough. There are not many marriages where the husband could kiss his wife and leave for his job any given day without her knowing where he was going, and then reappear six months later not saying where he had been or what he had been doing. Many such marriages don't last. McNab has been married five times.

But Sue was tough and she had a good sense of humour. She told us that she was often chatted up by men at the gym. She used to put them off by telling them 'my husband kills people for a living', and then explain that it was not a joke. But her toughness and sense of humour were being tested. While her husband was away Sue was followed to a supermarket by men in unmarked cars in an act of intrusive government surveillance, designed to intimidate. The word had been passed down that they were trying to financially ruin Coburn. (Later, they had to sign over the equity in their house for legal aid.)

The pressure was enormous. An email to us from Sue said Mike was worried he would be arrested at the airport while returning to the UK. Having given an interview to us, face to camera, Coburn changed his mind. He wanted to be disguised on camera and to withdraw parts of the interview. He wanted some of his criticism of British officers edited out and likewise some of the things he had said about other missions.

I received a grim message from him.

> *If this was simply my own head on the chopping block I would be less concerned, but with the way events have turned, the whole of my life is now under threat … Sue is physically sick with stress and worry at the moment and we are on the verge of capitulating, book and all, to the MOD. None of us expected this stress, none of us expected the contract to be so binding … it feels like someone has raped me, and taken away all my rights. All my good intentions for this project, doing right by everybody, seem to have fallen by the way. I must have been naïve to think my stand would make the situation right for everyone.*

I argued that his story was in the public interest, his criticism of British officers was fair comment, that the changes would sabotage the program and that the Ministry of Defence would not make any compromises even if he censored himself. It is not uncommon for people talking to journalists to get cold feet later and try to withdraw or change an interview. In Coburn's case it was perfectly understandable given the pressure he was under.

Was my first obligation to the source or to the story? The story was clearly in the public interest but my source faced having his life ruined. This was not a black and white question, more shades of grey. In the end, we stuck with a couple of age-old principles. First, that the duty of a journalist is disclosure and second, that the only way to assert the right to publish is to publish. To allow a government to decide what the media can or cannot publish, through pressure or otherwise, would be the end of a free press. Coburn and I parted company on this issue, much to my regret. We made some changes to the program and prepared to go to air.

The British government, however, tried to stop the *Assignment* program from being broadcast. It hired a large legal team, including New Zealand's most expensive QC. TVNZ mounted its own legal defence. Her Majesty's government lost in the New Zealand High Court. It lost in the Court of Appeal. It was refused leave to go to the Privy Council in the UK. The program went ahead.

But the UK government persisted. They fought a separate legal battle against the book. Coburn, assisted by a determined barrister, Warren Templeton, who had also represented Richard Tomlinson in his battles against the British government, won that round too and the book, *Soldier Five*, was published. But repeated defeats did not deter the British government, nor did the huge cost in British taxpayers' money.

Coburn was intending to distribute the proceeds of the book sales between the surviving members of the patrol, the families of those who died and the SAS association. He felt that it might have helped to make up for the wrong done to Vince Phillip's family. But the British government stopped that happening too. They eventually succeeded in the British courts in preventing Coburn from getting any royalties from the book, anywhere in the world.

The NZSAS outside their Killing House. And on patrol in the mountains.

■ ■ ■

Visit any bookshop, anywhere in the world, and look around the military and history sections. Title after title stacked on the shelves will be stories of or by special forces soldiers, from the SAS and SBS in the UK to Seal Team Six and Delta Force in the US. Visit the fiction section and you will find a whole genre of novels about special forces operators, many of them written by Andy McNab and Chris Ryan. The work of special forces soldiers, in truth and fiction, is now a publishing industry. The dam has burst, not only in the UK but also in the US and other countries. Attempts, judicial and otherwise, to enforce secrecy have failed. Seal Team Six members have written books about the mission to kill Osama bin Laden.

Bravo Two Zero is still a bestseller; there was even a twentieth anniversary edition available on Amazon for US$24. You can get Coburn's *Soldier Five* for just US$1.80.

Andy McNab is now a one-man industry, a brand, and has written a series of books featuring SAS characters Nick Stone and Tom Buckingham. He has written children's books. He has written two autobiographies. He also lectures to security and intelligence agencies in the US and UK, works in the film industry advising Hollywood on special forces procedures and in training actors to be like soldiers and he is a spokesman and fundraiser for both military and literacy charities.

McNab has been honoured by the Queen, with a CBE, Commander of the Order of the British Empire. Strangely, he has also written a book about psychopathy, *The Good Psychopath's Guide to Success*, having discovered he had psychopathic traits. *Bravo Two Zero*, his first book, has elements that are clearly fiction. There was no challenge by the British government, no briefing sympathetic journalists to undermine a version of events that they did not like. Instead the government stood back as the book was published and became a runaway success.

In contrast Coburn is still on 'the circuit', working in some of the world's most dangerous places, using his special forces skills to guard companies and their workers. He cherishes his anonymity. At one stage Coburn was based in a Kurdish-controlled area near the border with Syria, a few miles from territory controlled by the fanatics of ISIS. He has worked in a remote area of Papua New Guinea and in Nigeria, a place he describes as the most corrupt country he has ever been in. He now lives in Singapore but is no longer married to Sue.

The treatment of Coburn by the British government was outrageous. Confidentiality contracts may be necessary to stop leaks about current or planned missions but their use in this instance was an abuse of power. Coburn's attempt to give the public a different view of what happened on the famous patrol and to defend the reputation of fellow soldiers who could no longer defend themselves was an act of bravery.

It was very much in keeping with the SAS ethos, summoned up by the famous poem you can find in the regiments' church in Hereford:

We are the Pilgrims, master, we shall go always a little further:
It may be beyond that last blue mountain barred with snow,
Across that angry or that glimmering sea.
White on a throne or guarded in a cave
There lives a prophet who can understand
Why men are born: but surely we are brave
Who take the golden road to Samarkand.

ELEPHANT MAN: TRUTH SUPPRESSION EVEN UNTO DEATH

Special forces missions these days are the subject of books and TV dramas. Many special forces operators have followed in the footsteps of McNab/Mitchell. But most missions are still shrouded in secrecy. In particular, if the mission goes wrong and a soldier dies, the truth about what happened will be vigorously supressed. The grieving family of a special forces soldier is often left with many unanswered questions. The level of secrecy is especially high in the UK, Australia and New Zealand.

Dan Flanagan was in the New Zealand SAS and was killed in Zimbabwe, leaving behind a wife and two young children. Officially, he had gone to Zimbabwe with five other NZSAS men on a training exercise. Unofficially, he was working alongside British SAS units in an operation called Falcon Drum. The soldiers parachuted into the north of the country in a national park near Lake Kariba, an area targeted by gangs of heavily armed ivory poachers. Twenty-four hours later, Flanagan was dead, apparently trampled to death by a rogue elephant.

Flanagan's widow Leonia was given three different accounts of what happened: that he parachuted directly into a herd of elephants; that a herd stampeded into the tent he was lying in; that he and his partner disturbed a mother elephant and it charged them. The two men split up, the elephant followed Dan and killed him. After the incident, an SAS officer requested that no post mortem be carried out, according to a secret after-action report: 'OC D Squadron was advised by Captain Blackwell of the need to avoid a post mortem examination.'

Leonia Flanagan saw her husband's body after it was flown back to Auckland and she was surprised by his injuries. They did not seem to have been made by an elephant. His chest was punctured in four places by what she thought were bullet wounds. Rather than being the victim of an elephant, it looked like Lance Corporal Flanagan had been shot. It was a belief shared by some of his SAS colleagues, who said he had been shot while on a mission against the poachers. The army denied it and to this day Flanagan's death is still recorded as being an accident.

If there was a cover-up, what would be the motive? What are described as training missions for the New Zealand unit are often active operations, working alongside the British SAS and other special forces units. Governments of all stripes in Wellington have found it useful to maintain the ambiguity surrounding SAS deployments overseas.

9.

**From the toolbox:
Behind closed doors**

MAKING LOTS OF PEOPLE ANGRY IN THE WORLD'S FRIENDLIEST COUNTRY

IN THE NEWS, 20 MAY 2000

Mission Impossible II **tops US box office**
Danish climbers reach the summit of K2
How the ship went down; turmoil at Team NZ

The famous yachtsman Sir Peter Blake was angry and red faced. As I sat opposite him in an office he banged his fist repeatedly on the table. 'Not true, not true, not true,' he said. The office was at Westhaven in Auckland and outside the window you could see the forest of masts that made the area famous in the yachting world. It was a sunny day with blue skies. However, inside Blake's office it was getting hot and with each strike of the table I flinched and told myself what a fool I had been to agree to this meeting.

I was editor of the *New Zealand Herald*, the country's largest newspaper. A Kiwi team, Team New Zealand, had captured the America's Cup, the famous yachting trophy, and were defending it in Auckland, the City of Sails. The victory, by a team representing a nation of 4 million up against the wealth and technology of the United States, was a fantastic achievement. It had inspired the nation and defending the cup in Auckland was generating a mini-bonanza for the local economy.

Sir Peter Blake ran Team New Zealand with a ferocious single-mindedness and I admired him and his style of management, summed up in his motto: 'Will it make the boat go faster?' It was a question he asked team members who wanted to see him about a particular problem so as to get them to concentrate on the essentials. It seemed to me a good way to manage a large, complex operation — like the *Herald*, a six-days-a-week paper with a large circulation and a staff of nearly 200 people, the closest New Zealand had to a national newspaper.

Blake was angry because my reporters had written a story exposing splits within the team, revealing that there were bitter behind-the-scenes arguments about money and strategy. The *Herald* management at that time (it is now under different ownership) was keen that we not get offside with Team NZ. I was persuaded to go and see Blake and I had agreed. Blake spent some time denying the stories about trouble in the team — even though he and I both knew they were true.

But the overall message was clear: we were the hometown newspaper, we were expected to support the home team so no messy reporting about disputes the team was trying to keep hidden. Didn't

I support Team NZ? Wasn't I happy the Cup would be hosted in Auckland? I was. I am a proud Kiwi and a sporting nut. The America's Cup victory had brought money and prestige to Auckland and the *Herald* welcomed this. The paper celebrated the victory and the Cup's defence. But as editor and with my reporters, we were still determined to cover the Cup as a news story, fairly and accurately without fear or favour. Journalists understand the difference.

Boosterism — the act of promoting an organization, a town, a city or project with the goal of improving public perception of it — is practised by all media organizations. It's a part of the life of a journalist and it can be a curse. Despite what some of the public might think, journalists like good-news stories as well as bad. Journalists can cheer along with the public when our team wins. Journalists appreciate the merits of the city or country they are living in — particularly if it is somewhere reporters are not killed or jailed for doing their job.

Most media companies are privately owned and they need to make money to survive. There is no contradiction between this and doing your job. So the fiercely independent *New York Times* can promote the benefits of living in that great city while also highlighting crime and poverty and civic scandals. And the BBC, with its charter guaranteeing editorial independence, will still go over the top when a British tennis player wins Wimbledon. Transparency is the key — being honest with the viewing and reading public about why you are doing what you are doing.

But government organizations, corporations and other groups will often seek to avoid transparency by putting pressure on journalists behind closed doors or bypassing editorial staff altogether and appealing to the executives or boards of the media company that owns the newspaper, radio or TV station they are trying to influence.

The behind-closed-door tool can be deployed on truly momentous stories — such as the attempt to pressure *Washington Post* owner Katharine Graham to stop her newspaper publishing the Pentagon Papers, a secret history of the Vietnam War, as memorably portrayed in the Hollywood movie *The Post*. The very existence of the paper was under threat as it was borrowing money from the banks to expand at the time that the government was putting it under enormous legal pressure. Graham resisted the pressure and they published.

Or the tool can be brought into use in far less vital contexts, such as with the *NZ Herald* and Team NZ. The pressure can be personal or financial or both.

Sometimes the most trivial things will trigger its use. A local news event will often be sponsored and that sponsor could be an advertiser or organization that wants to influence coverage of the story. At one stage, the *Herald* failed to turn up for a rather minor event organized by the University of Auckland. We were going to run a story but without a photo. A complaint from a public relations man is a classic example of what can happen:

> *Adding to our frustration is the university did not arrange for their own photographer to cover (assuming they could access Herald pix) so we have nothing to fall back on. This is a double blow because we wanted to utilise photos for internal university publicity and also for business, education and sponsor/partner publications. I don't know how or whether there is some way of recovering this. Hood [John Hood, then university vice-chancellor, later Sir John, rose to be vice-chancellor of Oxford University] is furious and is demanding explanation etc. but he will cool down. At the very least if we could have been advised at least then I don't increase his and everyone else's expectations. There*

*was a whole team there from the uni and this reflects badly on [name
withheld]. As you are aware there is some tension around the project
and our failure to deliver will be seized upon internally.[1]*

So forget news value, this was pure public relations — we were to be
the providers of collateral for the university and we were expected to
feel sorry for the PR man who had made promises he couldn't keep.

ADVERTISING VS EDITORIAL

A common experience of every editor or media executive is to
be threatened by an advertiser. Before it migrated online, the
real estate industry was a huge advertiser in the mainstream
media. Real estate advertising was worth millions of dollars
a year to the *NZ Herald*. We ran a comment piece — not a news
story — criticizing some of the methods used at auctions. The
reaction was fierce. The letter below was sent to a *Herald*
executive, bypassing editorial. Note the claim that the public
can't tell the difference between opinion pieces and news —
and the clear threat at the end:

> *We continue to be astounded and extremely
> disappointed by the way in which the NZ Herald
> is denigrating the real estate industry, Thursday's
> massive article ... being the latest and worst example
> of this. We are fully aware of the requirement to keep
> editorial and advertising separate and we have never*

asked for or expected special editorial favours from the Herald because of our status as your biggest advertiser.

However, we are at a loss to understand why you should bite the hand that feeds you (in that most real estate display advertising is for no-price, auction properties) by giving huge prominence to such a nasty and vindictive article. We are appalled that an embittered, former real estate agent who spent only a short time in the industry should be given so much space to vent his spleen in the Herald and slag off the industry, and, in his second article, auction marketing in particular.

I know the standard Herald response will be that the Dialogue page is an 'opinion' page and everyone is free to express an opinion. This simply doesn't wash with us. Most people consider what they read in the paper to be fact. In this case, the article has little basis in fact and simply amounts to a venomous attack on auction selling and no-price marketing.

As you will appreciate we have been very loyal to the Herald over many years and we appreciate the very competitive deals and good service that ... [I have left out the name of the Herald advertising executive here; he was just doing his job] has provided us with in return. However as you are probably aware many of our offices are being approached by other media such as Property Press, NBR, Xtra and The Sunday Star Times who are very keen to get our business and

> *are offering very competitive rates to do so. You will*
> *also no doubt by now be aware of the general outrage*
> *among the industry over the article and that many*
> *agencies — including us — are seriously questioning*
> *our relationship with the Herald.[2]*

This is an example from my own journalistic history, but since then media publishers have seen their revenues plunge as advertising migrates online. Advertisers hold more sway than ever before in the shrinking world of print. Lines have blurred — note the now-common use of the appalling word 'advertorial'. This is not just history. Conversations like this behind-closed-doors pressure are going on at newspapers, radio and TV stations and online media all over the world.

Team New Zealand, after successfully defending the America's Cup in Auckland, fell apart, just as our reporting had predicted. As soon as the victory parades and parties were over and all the champagne had been drunk, the rows over cash, the shouting matches and duelling egos, burst into the open. Russell Coutts, the team leader, who had proclaimed that he wanted to establish a dynasty capable of retaining the America's Cup for 25 years, defected to a Swiss syndicate, along with other key team members. The Swiss took the Cup off New Zealand three years later, and the show left town.

We had written about the rift on the day of the first race of the first defence. Blake had said, on and off the record, that it was 'absolutely untrue'. Blake stood down from the team after the defence. He was shot and killed by pirates during an environmental expedition on the Amazon River a year later. By then I had left the

Herald, but not before a series of epic battles over journalistic ethics and editorial independence.

We were shaking things up — doing long investigative series on the banks and medical malpractice, about an American billionaire who had got off scot free (with his name supressed) after bringing marijuana into the country, and fighting in court to name a police officer involved in a controversial shooting. I was applying the principles I believed were essential for proper journalism that I had learnt as an investigative reporter in the UK and US and while part of the launch team of the *Independent on Sunday* in London, the first truly independent British national newspaper. *The Independent on Sunday* was owned by journalists and run by journalists for many years.

But the *Herald* was not. As the complaints piled up from the business community and the *Herald* management became increasingly nervous, I was about to meet my ultimate boss. Legendary Irish businessman and rugby super star Tony O'Reilly was visiting Auckland.

It was planned like a Royal visit. Preparations were made months in advance and we received a twelve-page itinerary listing the limo rides and hotel suites and speeches and dinners and the meetings with then Prime Minister Helen Clark and Winston Peters (now New Zealand Deputy Prime Minister) and leaders of the local business community.

The itinerary featured entries like this: '8.30am. Photo/ interview on the lawn at Thornton Lodge for *Bay of Plenty Times*. The paper is looking to run a story showing one of the world's greatest businessmen on their patch … it is not a heavy economic story. They would like you to share your favourite Irish joke with their readers.'

Also planned was an appearance at a lunch organized by the Auckland Chamber of Commerce. O'Reilly had brought with him a powerful friend, the former prime minster of Canada, Brian

Mulroney, who would deliver a speech to local VIPs on the benefits of free trade. O'Reilly and all the top management of the *Herald* would be present. I didn't pay much attention to this item. I should have.

O'Reilly had first come to attention as a dashing winger who toured New Zealand with the British and Irish Lions in 1959, scoring 23 tries in 22 matches and attracting a horde of female admirers. His business career was meteoric. He became chief executive of HJ Heinz and then chairman, the first non-family member to hold that position. He led the Independent News and Media group, which owned the *New Zealand Herald*. He had a reputation for not interfering in the news coverage of the papers he owned, which put him in a different category from the other two media magnates I had met during my career.

While working at a provincial British newspaper, *The Reading Evening Post*, I had led a classic local newspaper campaign — to stop the merger of Reading and Oxford football clubs into one club, the brainchild of Robert Maxwell, the press baron, owner of Oxford FC and also the *Daily Mirror*. Maxwell was a notorious bully who frequently sued journalists and other media groups if they printed things he did not like. During our campaign, I interviewed him and he tried to bully me. He actually went to the trouble of phoning me up and telling me he was going to buy the *Post* and sack me.

We had the last laugh. Maxwell had declared that opponents of the merger had as much chance of winning as they had of making the River Thames flow backwards. We used the quote prominently when it was announced that the campaign had succeeded and the proposed merger was dead in the water.

Later I briefly met Rupert Murdoch while he was visiting the canteen at *The Sunday Times* in London. The paper was under siege from striking print workers outside and Murdoch was making a morale-boosting visit. It was an awkward visit; Murdoch seemed uncomfortable and he left quickly.

Unlike Robert Maxwell and Rupert Murdoch, O'Reilly was charming and I was so taken in by this that at a small private dinner that included O'Reilly's top people and Mulroney, I spoke up and offered an alternative point of view to something he had just said. I quickly realized my mistake. The table fell silent and he reacted by glaring at me angrily. Seconds later, he was back to his charming self as if nothing had happened.

Brian Mulroney made his speech to the Auckland Chamber of Commerce that contained no great revelations and was a standard recital of the merits of free trade. We had a reporter there. Soon afterwards, the paper's editor in chief popped into my office to ask what we intended to do with the story. I said it was a business story and would go in the business section.

Later I had a visit from the chief executive of the paper who made it clear that 'Tony' wanted the story on the front page of the newspaper. I explained that it wasn't worth the front page as there was nothing new in it and that there were other more important stories that the paper was covering. He left, very unhappy. As the day went on, there were more messages and more visits. Tony was insisting that his friend Brian Mulroney's speech be given prominence on the front page and Tony would be very unhappy if this was not done.

It was a textbook example of behind-closed-doors pressure. It would have been easy to give in — it was a pretty innocuous story. But as the great comedian Jon Stewart once said, if you don't stick to your values when they are being tested, they're not values, they're hobbies. I stuck to my guns but by the end of the day I was exhausted and depressed, and I did not sleep that night.

WE GOT IT WRONG

Media organizations and journalists, with honourable exceptions, have tried to hide their mistakes. This is notable among the tabloids in print and TV versions. The belief is that to freely admit mistakes such as misquoting people, or muddling up facts, or a wrong photo, will damage credibility of the media organization. Often it takes legal action or a complaint to a press council or broadcasting standards authority to force a correction and then it is usually buried deep inside the newspaper or magazine or TV or radio bulletin.

But if we demand accountability and transparency of those we report on, then the media also needs to be accountable and transparent. To own up to error is simply to acknowledge that we are fallible. In doing so we will make ourselves more credible, not less. The public standing of journalists has declined dramatically. We need ways and means of restoring our standing, as reputable journalism is so vital. When I was editor of the *New Zealand Herald*, I decided to introduce an expanded corrections column and to call it 'We Got it Wrong'.

The company's marketing and advertising executives were horrified and held meetings to try to talk me out of the idea or at least give the column a less bold title. I felt 'We Got it Wrong' was perfect as we were being upfront and honest with our readers and, despite the opposition, went ahead. The day after I resigned from the *Herald*, the 'We Got it Wrong' column disappeared.

Behind-closed-doors discussions are often used by politicians, government officials and business leaders to prevent a story being told or, as in the case of the Mulroney speech, to promote a story well beyond its merits or to kill it. There can be appeals to the national interest, or commercial interests, or friendship. It can and does get deeply personal. I was once threatened by a senior police officer over our attempts to publish the name of a policeman involved in a shooting. On another occasion, I was told that a prominent businessman with close connections to the *NZ Herald* would kill himself if we published an investigation into allegations against his company.

Another behind-closed-doors tactic is to attempt to persuade you that the story you are about to publish is not true or is misleading. The problem then is that they are denying something but are not accountable for the denial, because the conversation is off the record. The off-the-record versus on-the-record rules are not well understood by the public, despite popping up in movies and crime dramas which, incidentally, are now are likely to portray journalists as sleazy characters with no morals — a far cry from the heroes that investigative reporters were on film and TV in the 1970s and 1980s. See Redford and Hoffman in *All the President's Men*.

Even journalists argue about the terms. On the record is easy — the information can be used, quoting the source, for publication or broadcast. Off the record means for most reporters that you can use the quote but not identify the source, but the Associated Press, in its guidebook, says it means the information cannot be used for publication. There are two other important terms — 'on background' means you have information, usually more than just a quote, which you have agreed with your source you can use while attributing it only in the most general terms, e.g. 'a White House source' or 'a Ministry of Defence official'. 'Deep background' is where you use the information but do not refer to the source in any way, not even in the most general terms.

These rules are important — they protect whistleblowers who want to reveal things that are in the public interest, and who face disciplinary action, dismissal, financial ruin, harassment of them and their family or even jail if they are found out. Without these rules there would be little investigative reporting and even less accountability in public life. But behind closed doors, the off-the-record rule is abused. Someone can deny a story even if it's true — and not be accountable for the denial.

Of course, it can be a mistake to think that the public is as interested as a journalist in all these high-minded matters. While I was battling for editorial independence at the *New Zealand Herald*, I found that many of our readers had other, less weighty concerns.

I received the following from one of our readers:

The Editor NZ Herald

Dear Sir,

Are you determined to get rid of all your regular readers?

If you think we buy your paper to read endless boring ads for cheap dishwashers and half-price dinner sets, you are much mistaken. We enjoy the historical reports and quotations; the cryptic crossword, even though it is printed so small that there is hardly room to write the answers; the bridge column when it made its brief weekend appearance; and above all Calvin and Hobbs ... to lighten the catalogues of mayhem and political conjuring tricks which make up the attenuated columns of news squeezed in between the advertisements.

During my editorship, we won awards, ran major campaigns, fought momentous legal battles and covered historic events. But the strongest reader reaction, by far, was when I cancelled the cartoon Calvin and Hobbes. I was roundly condemned. It was not the first time I had been accused of being out of step with public opinion.

What do you do when you are covering a warm and fuzzy whale rescue and you discover that it's all a con?

This Herald cartoon has pride of place on my office wall at home, reflecting our successful campaign to name an American billionaire who had been let off and had his identity protected after trying to import drugs into New Zealand. Young local men were identified and prosecuted for similar offences. It was a classic case of one law for the rich …

10. A different tool: Happy endings, deception practised by journalists and other good people

MISLEADING THE WORLD'S CHILDREN

IN THE NEWS, 5 FEBRUARY 2012

New York Giants defeat the New England
     Patriots in the Super Bowl
250 die in European cold snap;
     Russia reduces gas supplies
Whale movie *Big Miracle* grosses $2.7
     million in weekend box office

As darkness fell 4800 kilometres (3000 miles) north of the Arctic circle, Captain Arnold Brower drew on the local wisdom of the Inuit hunter to help persuade three whales to abandon an ice hole that had kept them alive for two weeks. A group of scientists, soldiers and oil industry workers had exhausted themselves as they cut the hole in temperatures as low as –40 °C (–40 °F) when the wind blew.

The three grey whales were ignoring all efforts to get them to move to a new breathing hole cut over 90 metres (100 yards) closer to the safety of open water. Every five minutes a 12.5-metre (40-foot) long whale nicknamed Crossbeak broke the surface, followed

Me at an ice hole in northern Alaska. With a whale.

by Bonnet and then Bone, the 8-metre (25-foot) baby of the trio. Each whale blew out twelve times before taking a deep breath and diving once more into the icy waters.

Even when rescuers covered the 8-metre (25-foot) hole with a tarpaulin, the whales refused to move, nuzzling the bottom of the canvas with their heads. The whales were bleeding from rubbing against the underside of the ice pack. If they couldn't be attracted to the new hole they would die. Rescuers had tried lights and the sound of a de-icing machine to move them on.

Arnold Brower had a better idea. He took a long wooden stick, leaned over the hole and tapped one of the whales with it. The three whales disappeared under the water and re-emerged seconds later in the new hole. I was gathered with media from around the world, over a hundred of them, in Barrow, Alaska, population 5000, only 1760 kilometres (1100 miles) from the North Pole. Three whales trapped in ice had turned into a major international story.

At Point Barrow, just outside town, a giant helicopter carrying a 4400-tonne (10,000-pound) concrete block cut into a sharp point by oil company engineers, had been punching holes in the 30-centimetre (12-inch) ice at regular intervals. The holes were supposed to help the whales across the 6.4 kilometres (4 miles) between where they were trapped and loose ice that offered an escape route to the Beaufort Sea. If they could be lured into the shifting ice they had a chance of going on their long-delayed 8000-kilometre (5000-mile) migration to the Arctic Ocean, through the Bering Strait and south — to their southern home in the warm waters off Baja, California. Their arrival had given the North Alaskan economy an unexpected boost as the media swarmed in, hiring light planes and snowmobiles and guides, and buying expensive extreme-weather gear.

The town had previously suffered an epidemic of alcoholism among the local Inuit and a major corruption scandal. Millions of dollars of federal aid intended to improve life for the Inuit had been skimmed off by businessmen — a small prefabricated school building had cost US$80 million, while US$600 million had been spent on underground utility pipes.

In this remote landscape there was now a surreal site of network satellite dishes scattered across the ice. Each night, Pepe's North of the Border, the world's most remote Mexican restaurant, was packed with hungry reporters. The Inuit were happy to pose for photos, charge guide fees to take the media out to the ice hole on snowmobiles and explain why we should steer well clear of polar bears.

Barrow was dry because of the booze ban introduced in response to the local alcohol problem, but that didn't stop the press. A group clubbed together to send a British reporter all the way back to Anchorage and he returned with a load of beer and whisky. On the US networks the story had superseded the 1988 US presidential election contest between Bush senior and Dukakis, and children worldwide were following the rescue, drawing pictures of the whales at school. Predictably, the whales had been given names — Putu, Siku and Kanik in Inuit, and English names Bonnet, Crossbeak and Bone.

Whales died in Alaska every year. For example, Inuit hunters killed Bowheads to supply heating oil, clothing and food for their families throughout the winter. Each year some of the 22,000 grey whales protected by law got trapped under the icepack and died. If the whales had been trapped just a kilometre or so further from the shifting mass of ice they would not have been found. But one morning a local hunter, Roy Ahmaogak, spotted the trapped greys beating themselves against the ice in a fruitless effort to break free.

No one knew why the whales got trapped. Perhaps they had wandered too far east to feed or maybe there were too many grey whales for the food supply, forcing some of them beyond the traditional feeding grounds and thus missing the migration to Mexico. A few greys died each season and washed up on the coast where they were stripped clean by polar bears. Many people felt that a rescue did not make sense. Jim Harvey of the National Marine Mammal Laboratory in Seattle told the media: 'That's natural mortality. The ones that make mistakes, the ones that are weaker, are the first that are going to die. And there is a reason for that. That's what keeps the population strong.'

Several Inuit sailing captains debated whether to shoot the three whales to put them out of their misery but instead agreed to try to save them. Roy Ahmaogak told people back in Barrow of the discovery but it scarcely warranted a mention in the community. There was a small item on the local cable television station news and the Anchorage newspaper ran a brief news story. Then a marine biologist contacted Cindi Lowry, the Alaska field representative of Greenpeace. She began working the phones and called the governor of Alaska, who happened to be in Barrow for a conference of state mayors. Lowry called US Senator Ted Stevens in Washington DC and she also alerted officials at the National Oceanographic and Atmospheric Administration, who gave her only a lukewarm response, asking whether the whales were important and about the cost of a rescue.

But Lowry persisted. She called the Alaska National Guard, congressmen and reporters. Eventually President Ronald Reagan offered to help save the whales and a huge US government-backed rescue effort got underway that included local oil companies. An oil services company dispatched a 185-tonne ice-crushing barge from Prudhoe Bay, 320 kilometres (200 miles) from Barrow. As the story spread it seemed that everyone in the area and across the whole Arctic wanted to get involved.

There was an excited announcement to the waiting media: 'The Russians are coming!' The Soviets, sensing a public relations opportunity, were sending two ships, the icebreakers *Admiral Makarov* and *Vladimir Arsenev*. The relationship between the Soviets and Greenpeace had been fraught. Greenpeace activists had been arrested after occupying a whaling station in Siberia and the Greenpeace ship *Rainbow Warrior* had to run from a Soviet freighter that tried to ram it in the Bering Sea. It took official calls from the State Department to Moscow to make it happen.

From the start of the rescue effort, Alaskans were ambivalent. Many of them thought the huge cost — US$500,000 in helicopter fuel alone — was a misplaced effort, especially in a local economy struggling with a worldwide slump in oil prices. David Grauman, a Barrow doctor, who had many patients who could not afford vital therapy tests and medication told me: 'There is overwhelming frustration in seeing enormous expenditures on behalf of these animals whilst being forced to watch our patients go without.'[1]

I wrote a story for *The Sunday Times* in the UK questioning the value of the rescue. But most of the media coverage reflected the excitement of children all over the world, much to the joy of Greenpeace. It was the sort of story people *wanted* to be true, and journalists were keen to go along with the deception. It appealed to our common humanity.

I confess that despite my story, every time I saw the whales appear in their ice hole I felt moved. It was hard to be neutral. Who could resist such a warm and fuzzy story — what parent had the heart to tell their children about natural mortality? All that was needed was a Hollywood-style happy ending. The whale called Bone stopped appearing in the ice hole. It was never seen again, presumed drowned. Children all over the world were in tears but there were still two whales who could be saved.

The Russian icebreakers cut a path to the ocean but the whales still refused to leave. The media was getting bored in Barrow and other stories started to compete for attention. Most reporters had already departed when the *Arsenev* made one final cut leading up to the latest breathing hole. As the sun came up, helicopters swooped over the ice and the sea, looking for the whales. They were gone.

The rescuers declared victory. The media reported that the whales had been saved and people got on with their lives. Barrow returned to normal and Pepe's North of the Border was once again serving its tacos and enchiladas to locals only. Greenpeace was happy with the publicity and the truth came a distant second.

The rescuers decided not to attach radio tags to the whales, which would have allowed them to be tracked but which had the potential for spoiling the happy ending the world demanded. The radio tags would have recorded, for instance, if the whales had simply been trapped by pack ice further out and died, away from all the cameras and the microphones. That was almost certainly their fate, according to the local hunters.

At a marine museum in Los Angeles, volunteers trained up so that they could identify the two remaining whales. The idea was that these volunteers in whale-watching boats would spot these missing whales at the end of their migration south. Whale program co-ordinator Larry Fukuhura told the Associated Press, 'We'll be copying the photos and giving lectures and hopefully we can spot them.' No sighting was made but a Hollywood movie was: *Big Miracle*, starring Drew Barrymore and John Krasinski. The movie plot was a romance set around the rescue and it reached the screens in 2012.

The most famous Mexican restaurant above the Arctic Circle caught fire in 2013 and despite a seven-hour effort by firefighters, little was left of Pepe's North of the Border.

■ ■ ■

Years later when I went back to review the story, I discovered to my horror that while we were all obsessed with the hyped-up and ultimately misleading whale rescue that wasn't, there had been a fire in Barrow. Three children, aged eight, two and ten months, had died when their flimsy house had burnt down. It had no smoke alarms and there were no adults present when the fire broke out. It should have been an important story about an isolated community battling social deprivation. But not a single word of this had appeared — on TV, radio or in print — anywhere else in the world the week it happened.

There is no such thing as a minor deception in reporting. We must report what is in front of us, even if it means a few unhappy children. The whale rescue coverage was a failure of journalism. We allowed ourselves to be distracted by the story when more important things were happening, locally and internationally. It is a failure that is repeated every day.

We, journalists and the public, are even more prone to distraction now — gravitating towards the simple human-interest tale with its YouTube-ready images at the expense of the more complicated, difficult and messy stories. Who wants to read a complicated story about banking or health care when you can watch a video of a car crash, in slow motion? We are still too busy watching the whales.

DECEPTION PRACTISED BY 'OUR SIDE'

Responsible journalism is under attack by President Trump and the right-wing media propaganda machine led by Fox News. Any story they do not like is now labelled with the infamous label 'fake news'. It is all too easy in such a febrile atmosphere to forget that some of the worst examples of truth prevention or distortion have come from the left and those lies, like those of the right, live on in cyberspace.

Few major stories have been surrounded by as much nonsense as the 9/11 attack, which has spawned at least twenty major conspiracy theories, each more unlikely than the last. A simple rule that investigative reporters know: human nature means it's hard to keep a secret even when small groups of people are involved. If the secret involves a politician, a group prone to leaks and gossip, it is even harder. Conspiracies like the 9/11 ones, which require hundreds or even thousands of people to keep a secret for many years, in government and out, are impossible.

One of the most blatant examples of propaganda, which you can still find being repeated online as a true story, came from documentary filmmaker Michael Moore, a hero of the left. In his movie *Fahrenheit 9/11*, by use of imagery and voiceover, Moore implied that President George Bush had approved a special flight to get relatives of Osama bin Laden living in the United States out of the country in the aftermath of the attack on the Twin Towers. And, he implied, this happened at a time that Americans themselves could not fly because their air space was closed to prevent new attacks from the air.

Further, the story suggested, allowing the family members to flee had prevented them from being questioned by officials and asked if they knew where bin Laden was, or whether they had had contact with him before or after the devastating attack. The implication was clear. The Bush White House didn't want the family questioned and they wanted them out of the country — maybe this was an early 9/11 cover-up?

Moore's piece was sophisticated propaganda in that he implied the story without stating it as a fact. He used newsreel footage of passengers stranded by the 9/11 grounding. The voiceover says: 'Who wanted to fly? No one. Except the bin Ladens.' That is followed by footage of a plane taking off, overlayed with the rock song *We gotta get out of this place*. Then the voiceover says, 'It turns out that the White House approved planes to pick up the bin Ladens.'[2]

The final report of the independent 9/11 commission made it clear that the FBI did question the relatives before they left — there were 22 interviews — and that the flight did not take place until much later than you would have thought from watching Moore's movie — a week after the airspace was open and US citizens could fly normally.

But Moore's propaganda was subtle compared with later advertisements produced by a fund run by leading Democrats who were trying to defeat President George Bush as he campaigned for re-election. A radio ad emphatically claimed that the bin Ladens had been allowed to fly 'when most other air traffic was grounded' and then stated, 'We don't know whether Osama's family members would have told us where bin Laden was hiding. But thanks to the Bush White House, we'll never find out.'

It said:

> *After nearly 3000 Americans were killed, while our nation was mourning the dead and the wounded, the Saudi royal family was making a special request of the Bush White House. As a result, nearly two-dozen of Osama bin Laden's family members were rounded up — not to be arrested or detained, but to be taken to an airport where a chartered jet was waiting ... to return them to their country. They could have helped us find Osama bin Laden. Instead the Bush White House had Osama's family flown home, on a private jet, in the dead of night, when most other air traffic was grounded.'*

It was in fact more convenient for the government to charter a flight — allowing all the bin Ladens to be questioned in one place, as opposed to intercepting them at a number of different airports. No evidence has ever been found implicating these family members in the attacks. But the story was widely believed — by more than 50 per cent of respondents in one poll, while among Democrats the figure was 70 per cent. Even a third of Republicans believed the story.

It was an early example of a 9/11 conspiracy theory. They have multiplied and entered the mainstream. Numbers of my students each year — future journalists — put their hand up when I ask who believes it was a conspiracy. The onward march of the conspiracies has not slowed, even when it is pointed out the various theories are mutually contradictory.

The damage has been done and while people are paying attention to those, they not looking at the many questionable things that governments are actually doing, in their name.

11. The assault on truth: Where to from here?

> Discrediting the media anywhere weakens it everywhere.
>
> — CONSERVATIVE COLUMNIST 2017

> The press is your enemy. Enemies. Understand that? … Because they're trying to stick the knife right in our groin.
>
> — PRESIDENT RICHARD NIXON, THE WATERGATE TAPES

> Mass propaganda discovered that its audience was ready at all times to believe the worst, no matter how absurd, and did not particularly object to being deceived because it held every statement to be a lie anyhow.
>
> —HANNAH ARENDT, *THE ORIGINS OF TOTALITARIANISM*

Fox News in the US is sometimes compared by its critics to *Pravda* in the old Soviet Union or the propaganda of Dr Joseph Goebbels in Nazi Germany. The comparison is unfair. The output of the Nazis and the Soviet Union was far superior in its ability to deceive than anything produced by Fox. In our current era, Vladimir Putin's Russia runs a sophisticated and successful program of disinformation via social media. It's hard to detect where a tweet or Facebook post comes from.

Fox News propaganda is much more simplistic and it's easy to work out the bits that aren't true. The same applies for propaganda from the left. Fact-checking is a feature of modern journalism and if you want to find out whether a statement is true or false, or a mixture of both, you usually can. But the question is, do enough people still care for there to be a backlash against the onslaught of lies and disinformation?

Polls worldwide show that many young people have lost faith in democracy. A significant number — up to a third, in some polls — do not agree that it's important to elect the people who govern. They don't trust the system any more because they have been lied to too often. Rather than a healthy scepticism, they have decided nothing can be believed and it follows that it does not matter whom you vote for or under what form of government you live.

In thirteen years I have taught more than 3000 journalism students from more than twenty countries and each year a significant number fail an introductory research exercise where they have to research a topic or a person online. Too many students are unable to distinguish between reliable and unreliable sources of information and between facts and speculation. They will happily report gossip and treat 'reality' TV as if it is real, failing to understand it is a series of selected clips of people performing for the cameras.

So the students — journalists of the future — are becoming adults in a world where we are producing more information each year than in the whole of human history and much of it is false and where they have lost faith in the only system of government that protects their freedom of speech.

It is not hyperbole to say there is a war on journalism, not just in Donald Trump's America but worldwide. But don't call it a war on journalism — it's a war on truth. Governments, politicians and corporations have always attacked reporting and reporters that they do not like. They were enemies, as in Nixon's infamous outburst when he was president (before he was forced to resign after journalists exposed extensive corruption in the Watergate scandal).

But now the attacks have a more sustained character. Discrediting the media was and is crucial to the political strategy that produced and sustained Donald Trump's presidency. Columnist Ron Unz, the former publisher of *The American Conservative*, explained in 2017: 'The media is the crucial force empowering the opposition and should be regarded as a primary target of any political strategy. Discrediting the media anywhere weakens it everywhere.'

The media is certainly in opposition, but only in the sense that its job is to challenge and hold accountable governments and others in positions of power. A report from Harvard Kennedy School's Shorenstein Center on Media, Politics and Public Policy analyzed news coverage of President Trump's first 100 days in office. The study was based on reporting in the print editions of *The New York Times*, *Wall Street Journal* and *The Washington Post*, the newscasts of CBS, CNN, Fox News, NBC and three European news outlets (the UK's *Financial Times* and BBC, and Germany's ARD).

The findings included:

President Trump dominated media coverage in the outlets and programs analyzed, with Trump being the topic of 41 per cent of all news stories — three times the amount of coverage received by previous presidents.

He was also the featured speaker in nearly two-thirds of his coverage. European reporters were more likely than American journalists to directly question Trump's fitness for office.

Trump has received unsparing coverage for most weeks of his presidency, without a single major topic where Trump's coverage, on balance, was more positive than negative, setting a new standard for unfavourable press coverage of a president.

Fox was the only news outlet in the study that came close to giving Trump positive coverage overall, however, there was variation in the tone of Fox's coverage depending on the topic.[1]

The media were doing their job as Trump's presidency had begun badly with few of his goals achieved in the first 100 days. But such reporting confirmed in the mind of Trump and his supporters that the mainstream media were the opposition. This meant they could be further demonized as people out to destroy his presidency.

These attacks work. They are amplified by social media and then the mainstream media dutifully reports the attacks on itself and so the abnormal becomes normal. Repeat the lie often enough and it becomes real for many.

Journalists have always attracted criticism and threats for doing their job. When I was editor of the *NZ Herald*, we ran a major series of pieces on then Labour Prime Minister Helen Clark's first 100 days in office. She had made a successful start and our reporting reflected that. But I was accused of being pro-Labour by the conservative National Party, and by some in the *Herald* management and the business community. (As it happens, I did not vote for or support either party, in that or any other election.)

The criticism comes with the territory and always seemed minor compared to the dangers faced by reporters in undemocratic countries. Russia murders journalists; Saudi Arabia sends hit teams to dismember columnists; Turkey locks them up in their hundreds; China controls them in an Orwellian system that has moved from censorship to thought control. But now our very role in society is being undermined, even in countries with a long tradition of freedom of the press. In recent polls in the US, up to two-thirds of Republican voters agreed with the statement from President Trump that journalists are 'an enemy of the American people'.

We have been slow in defending and explaining the value of journalism and too quick to abandon the traditional skills of reporting, lured by the siren song of social media. We have not adapted our ethical standards to the world of Twitter. When Trump and others make statements that are clearly false, for example, they are tweeted and shared by reporters as quotes: the President said today or claimed today, etc. It is not until the more detailed report appears on the media site or in a broadcast that you will read or hear — too late — how and why the statement is not true. Many more people will have read the tweet than the follow-up story. In this, we are simply aiding and abetting the spread of falsehoods.

But most of the blame lies with the increasingly successful deployment of the tools of truth suppression, made easier by our short attention spans. So the volumes of false information flowing around the world, both deliberate and unwitting, have combined with an unwillingness to accept actual facts and the demonizing of the media as opponents. These are elements leading us to disaster. Many experts, such as General Michael Hayden, former head of both the CIA and the NSA, believe we are already in the post-truth era. The winners in this are autocrats in Russia, China, Turkey and many other countries; would-be autocrats in democracies; and unscrupulous government officials and corporations all over the world who have something to hide. We will be the losers, unless we start to pay more attention.

We must start to treat information with the care it deserves, whether in our private lives or as citizens. We must take responsibility for the information we share. Do we really all want to be part of a long chain of people spreading lies around the globe?

We can also teach our children to be intelligent consumers of information, to understand the difference between fact and opinion, to understand that gossip is just that, and to be prudent in what information they share on social media or in person. Let's teach them to be less quick to come to an opinion, to ask more questions before making up their minds, and to realize that the complex problems of our planet can't be explained in a tweet or YouTube clip.

Thanks

No reporter works in isolation. From editors who approved the expensive and risky trips to research my stories, to cameramen who shot the images that made people pay attention, every story in this book was the result of teamwork. The book also draws on the fine reporting of journalists working for other media organizations.

Among the many who have assisted my investigations, I need to single out a few: Peter Wilby, former editor of *The Independent on Sunday* and the *New Statesman*, a great editor, reporter and friend; Terence Taylor, who as executive producer at TV3 backed some of my bolder investigations when others wouldn't, and New Zealand television reporter Rod Vaughan, who worked on some of these investigations with me.

I would also like to thank my former colleagues on the Insight team of *The Sunday Times*; Edward Lucas of *The Economist*, a true expert on Russia; Eamon Hardy and George Entwistle for their support during their time at the BBC; Sharon Fergusson of Television New Zealand, James Gardiner, formerly of the *NZ Herald*, and Mike McRoberts of TV3 in New Zealand.

A number of fine journalism students have assisted with research over the years: Rachel Slack, Rebecca Magill, Alice Bhandhukravi and Madeleine Lindh at the University of Arts London and Andrew Leeson, Bene Earl, Victoria Cotman, Natasha Chadwick and Thea Carley at Macleay College in Sydney.

The nature of investigative reporting means that you sometimes need the help of a good lawyer. I have been fortunate to work with some fine ones. London solicitor Akhtar Raja — a man interested in justice above all — was a great help throughout the human shields project. In New Zealand, William Akel and Phillipa Muir of Simpson Grierson offered tremendous support and expertise.

I must also mention public relations professional Jenni Raynish, who put principle ahead of profit.

Gareth St John Thomas, my publisher at Exisle, helped inspire this book and gave me expert guidance along the way, and Anouska Jones at Exisle provided superb support.

Many sources risked a lot to help with the stories in this book. Without such concerned and principled citizens, investigative reporting would not exist. In particular I owe a debt of gratitude to those in the military and intelligence communities who risked their careers so the truth could be told. To them, warriors and spies, I hope I have rewarded your trust.

To my darling daughters, Shannon, Katya and Iona, I hope you will grow old in a world where good journalism is still practised.

Finally, this book could not have been written without the constant support and encouragement of my wife Penny. I owe her more than I can ever repay.

Endnotes

Introduction
1. Snyder, T. (2017), *On Tyranny: Twenty lessons from the twentieth century*, The Bodley Head, London.

Chapter 1
1. Tomlinson, R. (2001), *The Big Breach*, open source publication; and interview with the author.

2. Norton-Taylor, R. 'MI6: The nightmare scenario as a rogue agent goes public', *The Guardian*, 13 May 1999.

3. 'Playing I Spy with Tomlinson', Joshua Rozenberg, BBC News, 20 May 1999.

Chapter 2
1. Leonel, M. (1992), *Roads, Indians and the Environment in the Amazon: From Central Brazil to the Pacific Ocean*, (translation from Portuguese by Edda Frost and Sam Poole), IWGIA, Copenhagen.

Chapter 3
1. Paul Barney, interview with the author.

2. Sveriges Television interview, 30 November 2004.

3. The investigation of transport of defence equipment on M/S *Estonia* January 2005, Swedish government.

Chapter 4

1. Macleay College school of journalism research interview, 2014.
2. Sajko inquest, Glebe Coroners Court, New South Wales, June 2014.
3. New South Wales Coroners finding, September 2014.

Chapter 5

1. From files of Department of Justice, Washington, January 2018.
2. Goodwin, M. 'Evidence suggests a massive scandal is brewing at the FBI', *New York Post*, 23 January 2018.
3. Harding, L. 'Deny, distract and blame: How Russia fights propaganda war', *The Guardian*, 3 May 2018.
4. Applebaum, A. 'The fake news Russians hear at home', *Washington Post*, 4 May 2018.
5. Dickerson, C. and Haag, M. 'FBI finds no evidence of attack in death of border agent', *New York Times*, 7 February 2018.
6. Prier, J. 'Commanding the trend: Social media as information warfare', USAF, *Strategic Studies Quarterly*, winter 2017.

Chapter 6

1. Interview with author and Television New Zealand reporter Rod Vaughan, 1998.
2. Prime Minister Margaret Thatcher, statement to House of Commons, London 6 September 1990.
3. Letter from Prime Minister John Major to Labour MP John Prescott, 2 October 1992.

Chapter 7

1. National Science Foundation Antarctica audit, July 2015.
2. Johnson, N. (2005), *Big Dead Place*, Feral House, Port Townsend, Washington.
3. Jones, O. 'Let's be honest: We ignore Congo's atrocities because it's in Africa', *The Guardian*, 6 March 2015.

Chapter 8

1. Quotes and information in this chapter come from various interviews with the author and TV reporter and colleague Rod Vaughan.
2. Report from NZSAS Group, 15 June 1995.

Chapter 9

1. Letter of complaint to *New Zealand Herald* management from public relations firm (name withheld).
2. Letter of complaint to *New Zealand Herald* management from real estate industry.

Chapter 10

1. Interview with author, Barrow, Alaska, October 1998.
2. Michael Moore documentary *Fahrenheit 9/11*.

Chapter 11

1. Study from Harvard Kennedy School's Shorenstein Center on Media, Politics and Public Policy, May 2017.

Picture Credits

All photographs by Stephen Davis, with the exception of:

Page 36, *New Zealand Listener* magazine.

Page 84, courtesy of the Sajko family.

Page 128, courtesy of the Chappell family.

Page 133, courtesy of John Nash.

Page 146, unknown.

Pages 153 and 154, Michael Lacoste.

Pages 164 and 165, Grahame Sydney.

Page 175, Jessica Barder.

Page 202, from the archives of NZSAS.

Index